THE RESILIENT PATH

TURNING UNCERTAINTY INTO STRENGTH

Discovering Inner Power Through Failure, Reflection, And Mindfulness

YADAVALLI SUBRAMANYAM

STARDOM BOOKS

www.StardomBooks.com

STARDOM BOOKS
112 Bordeaux Ct.
Coppell, TX 75019, USA

Copyright © 2024 by Yadavalli Subramanyam

All rights reserved. No part of this book may be reproduced or used in any manner without written permission of the copyright owner except for the use of quotations in a book review.

FIRST EDITION MAY 2024

STARDOM BOOKS, LLC.
112 Bordeaux Ct. Coppell, TX 75019, USA

www.stardombooks.com

Stardom Books, United States
Stardom Alliance, India

The author and publishers have made all reasonable efforts to contact copyright holders for permission and apologize for any omissions or errors in the form of credits given. Corrections may be made to future editions.

**THE RESILIENT PATH
TURNING UNCERTAINTY INTO STRENGTH**
Discovering Inner Power Through Failure, Reflection, And Mindfulness

Yadavalli Subramanyam

p. 118
cm. 13.5 X 21.5

Category: SEL027000
Self-Help: Personal Growth - Success
ISBN: 978-1-957456-47-8

DEDICATION

To my beloved mother and father, whose unwavering love and support have been my guiding light throughout this journey.

To my cherished wife, Dr. Sreedevi, whose boundless patience and understanding have sustained me through countless trials and tribulations.

To my precious daughter and son, Maitreyi and Vishwanath, who inspire me every day to strive for excellence and leave a legacy worthy of their admiration.

To my mentor and insightful philosopher, Dr. Sangita Reddy, whose belief in my potential has propelled me forward even when doubt lingered.

This book is dedicated with heartfelt gratitude to all who have contributed to shaping the story of my life.

CONTENTS

	Acknowledgments	i
	Foreword	iii
	Introduction	1
1	Embracing Fear: Understanding Its Power	5
2	Embracing Failure: A Path to Growth	17
3	Nurturing Positivity: Helping Yourself and The Society	27
4	The Power of Self-Reflection: Discovering Your True Potential	39
5	Cultivating Resilience: Bouncing Back from Setbacks	51
6	Mindful Living: Finding Balance and Inner Harmony	63
7	Embracing Change and Growth: Unlocking Your Potential	71
8	Charting Your Course: Setting and Achieving Meaningful Goals	83
9	Women as Mirrors of Success	93
	Conclusion	103
	About The Author	105

ACKNOWLEDGMENTS

Writing a book is not a solitary endeavor; it is a collaborative effort fueled by the support, encouragement, and guidance of numerous individuals and institutions. As I reflect on the completion of this work, I am deeply grateful to all those who have contributed to its realization.

First and foremost, I extend my heartfelt gratitude to the dedicated team at Stardom Publishers, whose unwavering commitment to excellence and professionalism has been instrumental in bringing this book to fruition. Their passion and dedication to the craft of publishing have been genuinely inspiring.

I am indebted to the numerous mentors and advisors who have generously shared their wisdom, insights, and expertise throughout my journey. Their guidance has been invaluable, shaping my perspective and enriching the content of this book.

I offer my deepest appreciation to my family and friends whose unwavering love, support, and understanding have sustained me through the highs and lows of the writing process. Their belief in me has been a constant source of motivation and inspiration.

Finally, I extend my heartfelt thanks to the readers who embark on this journey with me. I sincerely hope this book inspires, educates, and empowers you, enriching your lives and guiding your paths in your chosen field.

FOREWORD

In the narrative of personal growth and professional excellence, Mr. Subramanyam Yadavalli's journey stands as a beacon of inspiration and a testament to the human spirit's indomitable resilience. As the CEO of Apollo Hospital, his transition from a ward boy to a visionary leader in healthcare is not just a story of rising through the ranks but a powerful narrative on the essence of embracing fear, conquering failure, and the relentless pursuit of excellence. It is with great admiration and respect that I introduce his book, which is a compelling amalgamation of personal anecdotes, professional wisdom, and practical advice for anyone aspiring to transform their lives and careers.

This book delves deep into the heart of personal development, exploring themes that are universally relevant yet deeply personal. From understanding the power of fear to embracing failure as a stepping stone to growth, Mr. Yadavalli offers insights that are both profound and actionable. His chapters on nurturing positivity, the power of self-reflection, and cultivating resilience are not only reflective of his personal philosophy but also embody the principles that have guided Apollo Hospitals' ethos under his leadership.

Mr. Yadavalli's narrative is enriched by his unique perspective on mindful living, embracing change, and thriving in a fast-paced world. These chapters are a testament to his holistic approach to leadership and personal well-being, highlighting the delicate balance between professional commitments and personal fulfillment. His journey encourages us to look inward, to find balance and inner harmony amidst the chaos of our external environments.

The conclusion of this book is not just a summary of key teachings but a clarion call to action. It inspires readers to take the reins of their lives, to cultivate resilience, and to live with purpose and fulfillment. Mr. Yadavalli's personal story, combined with his insights on personal growth, offers a roadmap for anyone looking to embark on a journey of self-discovery and transformation.

In today's world, where fear and failure often deter individuals from pursuing their dreams, Mr. Yadavalli's book emerges as a guiding light. It is a reminder that the path to personal and professional success is paved with challenges, but it is through conquering these challenges that we find our true potential.

I am confident that this book will inspire, motivate, and guide readers across the globe to embrace their journey with courage and resilience. Mr. Yadavalli's life story and the lessons he shares are a powerful testament to the fact that every individual has the potential to achieve greatness, irrespective of their starting point.

Dr. Sangita Reddy
Joint Managing Director, Apollo Hospitals
Group Chair - G20 Empower, India & Past President – FICCI

INTRODUCTION

Life spans just a few fleeting decades. The initial ten years are spent in the bliss of childhood, largely unaware of what the future holds. As you segue into the second decade, you become increasingly attuned to society's expectations and the world's demands. By the close of the third decade, you're generally expected to settle on a career, a choice that typically lasts a lifetime, whether this decision is made with profound understanding, sheer instinct, or simply by drifting is a matter of individual choice.

Some of us have the clarity to pursue what truly resonates with our heart's calling. However, many grapple with the arduous task of discovering and then committing to that passion. The choice often oscillates between compromising on one's true calling and braving a transformative journey fraught with challenges. We observe some who make concessions while others combat nearly every obstacle. There are those who opt for the safer, more predictable paths, and then there are the audacious few who, time and again, take bold leaps of faith.

Mr. Yadavalli Subramanyam epitomizes this latter group. He persistently made those daring choices, aiming not just for personal growth but for the upliftment of his people, his organization, and the larger society. *"True ascent is achieved only when efforts are channeled towards nurturing your people and the organization,"* he opines. His trajectory, from a ward boy in a Hyderabad CT Scan center to the CEO of a prestigious healthcare organization in that very city, is as much a testament to his indomitable spirit as it is brimming with valuable life lessons. Navigating through myriad fears and embracing multiple failures, he managed to cultivate a positive mindset and an unyielding resilience to surmount the odds. Before we delve into Mr. Subramanyam's rich tapestry of insights and experiences, let's familiarize ourselves with his extraordinary journey.

Before the digital age transformed our perceptions, the prevailing wisdom for the preceding generations was straightforward: undergo formal schooling, proceed to college, and then make the inevitable choice between engineering and medicine. Decisions hinged on grade reports, parental expectations, and the all-important financial constraints. Without a solid educational background or impressive grades, there was scant awareness or aspiration for unconventional careers. The concept of 'pursuing passion' wasn't as much of a rallying cry for the youth as it is today.

At fifteen, Mr. Subramanyam experienced the biting sting of this old-world system. Falling short of clearing his matriculation (10th class) exams by the narrowest of margins, he briefly teetered on the precipice of despair, even contemplating ending his life. In that era, matriculation was often seen as the first genuine benchmark of one's potential. Those who couldn't clear it were swiftly branded as 'no-gooders' — a label that carried the weight of a lifelong sentence. Such a setback, especially against the backdrop of his middle-class roots, was crushing. With his aspirations anchored in the medical field, this detour was especially jarring.

However, fate, intertwined with a spark of resilience, intervened. That year, in a fortuitous turn of events, the state government granted five grace marks to students on the cusp of passing.

For Mr. Subramanyam, this was a pivotal moment, a realization that time could indeed heal and that after the darkest hours, dawn inevitably follows.

A few years later, Mr. Subramanyam faced another setback. Despite his best efforts and investing his father's hard-earned money into coaching, he didn't secure a medical seat after the entrance examination. This was a wake-up call, highlighting the potential limitations of his resources. Yet, he wasn't ready to relinquish his dream entirely.

Subsequently, he enrolled in a local college for an undergraduate degree. Coinciding with this was his father's retirement from the electricity board, which added financial strains to their household. The onus of contributing financially meant that Mr. Subramanyam had to strike a balance between academics and employment. In retrospect, he sees this period as his initiation into the gritty world of enterprise.

Capitalizing on his father's connections, he secured a contract to paint electricity poles in a particular Hyderabad district. Managing a team of daily-wage workers, he juggled supervising this project with college commitments, turning a profit in the process. However, this venture wasn't without its challenges.

A traumatic incident occurred when one of his workers suffered a fatal heart attack on duty. This tragedy introduced him to the complexities of crisis management, as he faced an anguished crowd holding him accountable for the worker's death. This ordeal, while distressing, also served as a valuable learning experience during his formative years, which will be explored in depth in subsequent chapters.

Despite completing his graduation, Mr. Subramanyam's passion for medicine remained undimmed. His degree didn't align with healthcare, yet when presented with a stable government job opportunity, he chose a different path. Opting to join a CT Scan center as a ward boy was a decision emblematic of his audacity and self-belief. This center was notable, being the sole facility equipped with a CT scanner in Hyderabad and the wider Andhra Pradesh (United) State at the time.

His innate fascination with medicine propelled him to rapidly assimilate the technicalities of CT scans. In no time, he progressed from a ward boy to a CT Scan technician. But for Mr. Subramanyam, this was merely a steppingstone, not the final destination.

Mr. Subramanyam swiftly built a reputation for himself through his initiative and dedication. He actively liaised with doctors across multiple hospitals and ensured he was always available for emergency scans. Leveraging the medical knowledge he had garnered, he not only performed scans but also detailed their medical implications to doctors, sometimes even remotely assisting those at their clinics or homes. Such initiative propelled his recognition within the medical community and earned him a promotion to a marketing role within his organization.

Embarking on another ambitious leap, Mr. Subramanyam ventured to establish his own Diagnostic center. During this phase, he also embraced the joys of family life, welcoming a daughter into the world. Yet, he soon recognized that while his professional life thrived, it was at the expense of quality family time. In a defining moment, he proactively approached Mrs. Sangeetha Reddy, the then-CEO of Apollo Hospitals.

This pivotal encounter reshaped Mr. Subramanyam's career trajectory. Under Mrs. Reddy's mentorship, he initiated several groundbreaking programs in the Indian medical realm, garnering numerous accolades. Climbing the organizational ladder, he eventually assumed the role of Regional CEO of Apollo Hospitals for both Telangana and Andhra Pradesh. Today, he oversees 10 Apollo hospitals and a medical college.

Mr. Subramanyam's journey is a tapestry of trials, tribulations, and triumphs. His experiences offer invaluable insights for anyone aspiring to realize their dreams. In this book, he delves deep, elucidating how he tackled fears, embraced setbacks, nurtured a positive mindset, and cultivated the resilience to face life's myriad challenges. By immersing in Mr. Subramanyam's narrative and embracing the wisdom he imparts, readers will be better poised to navigate their challenges and chart their unique paths to success. Enjoy the journey through these pages!

1
EMBRACING FEAR: UNDERSTANDING ITS POWER

Fear, particularly in the context of the middle-class Indian psyche, remains a potent deterrent to dreaming big, even from a young age. Despite the strides our society has made over the past few decades, this sentiment largely holds true across vast swathes of the country. This fear, often instilled from every conceivable direction, persistently shadows one throughout life. Anything beyond a conventional, average life appears daunting and seemingly unattainable through stellar academic achievement. This apprehension influences our choices, especially when it comes to investing in higher education or specialized training.

Moreover, this ingrained fear often inhibits us from venturing beyond our comfort zones, even if it means pursuing our true passions. When conditioned from a young age to be wary of the uncertain future, overcoming such deeply-seated fears becomes an uphill task.

Without the benefit of sound guidance to discern between irrational and rational fears, navigating one's way out of this entangled web of apprehensions can be challenging. Only with conscious effort and guidance can one muster the courage to take that leap of faith, believe in oneself, and seize the opportunities that life presents.

My Encounters with Fears

I hail from a humble village background. Among my family members, only my father received a formal education, hardly sufficient to land him a job in the electricity department. The rest, including his siblings and extended relatives, relied on their knowledge of Vedic scriptures and Upanishads, imparting these teachings throughout our Nandigama village and neighboring regions in Krishna District.

Though my origins trace back to this village, due to my father's job, we soon relocated to Hyderabad. There, my academic journey began at a local government school, where education was as intermittent as seasonal rains. Given the financial constraints, stemming from my father's modest earnings that supported not only our immediate family but also our relatives visiting the city, the small community government school was our only viable option. The school, lacking infrastructure with limited rooms and absent benches, left us with no choice but to study under the expansive shade of trees – rendering our studies "seasonal."

Despite these challenges, I reveled in the simplicity and joy of life. The gravity of academic milestones didn't dawn upon me until I approached the pivotal 10th class (matriculation) board exam. Back then, clearing this exam was a significant achievement. It acted as a litmus test, determining a student's academic worth. Failure at this juncture often invited societal disdain, labeling the student as a failure. Relatives would often write off any prospects for such a student. However, through a stroke of fortune, I barely passed, courtesy of a 5-mark grace awarded by the State government, intended to boost that year's low pass rates.

But this reprieve took its time, and society had cast its judgment on me in the interim. The label of 'failure' began to weigh on me, cultivating a growing dread about my future prospects. Still young and impressionable, I couldn't process or navigate these looming fears. At that age, philosophical introspection is rare. One needs to be more aware of the unfolding events and the reasoning behind them.

So, that was my first major failure in life. All my friends in the neighborhood went to good colleges after clearing matriculation. But I kept struggling for weeks. Why couldn't I clear the exam? Why couldn't I learn the subjects? Why couldn't I go to a good school like my friends? Why am I not able to speak in English? There were so many questions in my mind. The atmosphere around me felt very toxic, with my own parents, brothers, relatives, and everybody else amplifying the situation with their words.

But the questions kept growing in my mind, and with them, the fears as well– "What should I do next? How do I go forward? What would happen if I can't reach the next phase of life? I can't bear that shame. I have to end my life here. That's it. I will end my life. There will be no problem." That's the darkest place where my thought process had reached one day. But something stopped me from taking the extreme step.

In retrospect, it could again be the strength of my family and people around me or an internal belief that I can still do something. That day, fortunately, passed without an eventuality, and I continued to the next failure while fearing the future on and off. I was not aware of any other options besides mainstream studies. So, I felt that the entire world was against me. That was my major internal fear, and I couldn't understand how to deal with it. Fears can manifest into a nasty thought process if you can't handle it the way it should be addressed. My fears continued until I took on them later in my life when I found out what my purpose was.

Finding Purpose in Life

When facing the adversities of life, it's easy to fall into the abyss of pessimism and hopelessness. Often, our upbringing and societal pressures don't prepare us for the inevitable setbacks and disappointments that we will encounter. Our minds are wired from an early age to perceive failure as a sign of inadequacy rather than a natural course of existence. This perspective skews our perception, causing us to fixate on the negative aspects of our lives. In doing so, we create a mental barrier that obscures the potential opportunities lying ahead.

During such tumultuous times, the guiding light of a mentor, a guru, becomes indispensable. As beautifully explained, a guru's role is to illuminate the obscured path, shedding light on the potential within us. The term 'Guru,' rooted in ancient Sanskrit, perfectly encapsulates this essence. While 'gu' represents the enveloping darkness of our fears, 'ru' signifies its dispelling force. Thus, a guru, in the truest sense, acts as a beacon, guiding us through our internal tempests.

I discovered the transformative power of this guidance during a pivotal phase of my life. Upon visiting Ramakrishna Math and immersing myself in the profound wisdom of Indian philosophy, I was bestowed with clarity. The teachings transcended beyond mere words, instilling in me a renewed sense of purpose and determination. They taught me to perceive fear not as an oppressive force but as a veil that could be lifted with the right perspective.

This realization was groundbreaking. It made me discern that fear wasn't an impenetrable wall but a mist that could be navigated with determination and the right mindset. Instead of an end, fear was a pause – a moment of reflection, allowing one to evaluate and adapt. It was an invitation to reassess our goals, to broaden our horizons, and to muster the courage to dream bigger than before. Through this newfound perspective, fear transformed from a debilitating entity to a catalyst, propelling me toward uncharted territories and unforeseen success.

The journey to Ramakrishna Math, both literally and figuratively, became a turning point in my life. It wasn't just about understanding the philosophical teachings but internalizing them and applying them in practical life scenarios. The stories of stalwarts like Gandhiji provided a living testament to the profound power of transforming fear into fuel for change. His life was a prime example of how one can turn adversities into steppingstones.

Mahatma Gandhi's journey from being a barrister in South Africa to becoming the leader of India's independence movement was filled with numerous challenges.

His experience on that fateful night in Pietermaritzburg station wasn't an isolated incident of racial discrimination; it was a reflection of a deeply rooted systemic issue. But instead of succumbing to anger or despair, Gandhiji channeled his emotions to initiate a non-violent resistance movement against racial oppression. His resilience and steadfastness exemplified the power of viewing fear not as a constraint but as a compelling force for change.

Drawing inspiration from such tales, I began to reshape my perspective on fear. I realized that fear, in essence, is not an adversary but a companion, constantly challenging us to evolve and grow. Just like the dark goggles that obstruct our vision, our fears often distort reality, painting a bleak and disfigured picture. But once we summon the courage to confront them, the world reveals itself in all its brilliance.

The teachings I imbibed from Ramakrishna Math not only gave me insights into managing my personal fears but also provided lessons in leadership and management. I learned the value of collaboration, effective communication, and the importance of seizing opportunities. These were lessons not found in textbooks but gathered from real-life experiences and introspection.

Embracing fear was not about eliminating it but learning to dance with it. It was about harnessing its energy to push boundaries, to venture into uncharted territories, and to continually strive for personal and professional growth. It was a lesson in turning challenges into opportunities, failures into steppingstones, and fears into inspirations.

There is no Comfort Zone!

This profound understanding of life's ebbs and flows is reminiscent of the ancient teachings of the Bhagavad Gita, which discusses the transient nature of life and emphasizes the importance of self-awareness, duty, and continuous growth. Life is not static; it's dynamic and ever-changing. The concept of the "comfort zone" is a human-made construct that often serves as a self-imposed prison, limiting our potential and growth.

Drawing an analogy with the clock is apt. Just as the clock's hands are in perpetual motion, life never truly stands still. Stagnation, in any form, can lead to regression. While it's essential to cherish moments of calm and respite, it's equally important to recognize that these moments are fleeting. Challenges, setbacks, and trials are inevitable, but they also provide invaluable lessons and opportunities for personal evolution.

The fear of the unknown often holds us back. We tend to avoid change or new challenges because of the perceived risks. However, as highlighted, these very challenges can catalyze growth, transformation, and success. By embracing them head-on, with a spirit of curiosity and resilience, we can convert adversities into assets.

The differentiation between external and internal growth is vital. While society often measures success by external factors like wealth, status, or titles, true success and contentment come from internal growth and evolution. The pursuit of passion, purpose, and personal growth brings a sense of fulfillment unmatched by materialistic gains.

Moreover, it's crucial to understand that contentment and ambition aren't mutually exclusive. One can be content with their present situation while simultaneously striving for higher goals and betterment. It's this delicate balance that often leads to a fulfilled and meaningful life.

Thus, life's journey is not about seeking perpetual comfort but about embracing growth, challenges, and learning. It's about understanding that comfort zones, while reassuring, can be limiting.

By pushing boundaries, taking risks, and following one's passion, we can achieve not just external success but also internal satisfaction and peace.

Address Your Fears

If you aren't striving to evolve or improve, fears, whether acknowledged or not, are holding you back. It's essential to pinpoint these fears and address them directly. At times, you might be in denial or conceal them under the guise of comfort or guilt. Ignoring these fears can amplify them over time, looming as impending failures. Thus, it's crucial to confront and work on these fears daily, preventing the recurring struggle of rising from setbacks.

Today's youth are fortunate to be surrounded by a plethora of opportunities. It's up to them to confront their fears, embrace risks, and make judicious choices to carve their journey. Progression is vital because change remains life's only constant. With every ticking second, we age, and the inevitability or fear of death approaches. But this is a fact of life, a reality that doesn't warrant our fear. Instead of being paralyzed by such fears, especially one as profound as mortality, we should embrace life's uncertainties, acknowledging our limited time and striving to live our best lives. This perspective holds true for all concerns, most of which pale in comparison to the existential fear of death.

A straightforward yet impactful practice to enhance personal growth is dedicating 15 minutes to introspection before bedtime. This routine, a cornerstone of my personal journey, entails revisiting the day's events, reflecting on your actions, and distinguishing between positive and negative choices. By honestly assessing your day-to-day experiences, you can discern your triumphs and setbacks. Further introspection can help identify underlying fears or barriers, whether they be personal inefficiencies or external influences. Recognizing these factors is pivotal for self-improvement. Regularly engaging in this sincere self-dialogue can yield insights into genuine achievements, areas of growth, potential opportunities, and planning strategies for the forthcoming day. In many ways, this 15-minute daily reflection can be as transformative as a rigorous gym session, yoga, or meditation. It fosters mental tranquility and provides a foundation for continuous personal development.

Understanding one's fears is just the beginning. Venturing through the daunting maze of these fears often reveals a beacon of hope and clarity at the end. Hence, fears can be instrumental in fostering self-awareness and equipping you to navigate the world more adeptly. Youth, with its reservoir of vigor and adaptability, offers an opportune phase to confront and harness these fears as catalysts for growth. Challenging fears can morph them into formidable motivators, propelling you towards unparalleled heights. Conversely, remaining ensnared in the delusions of a comfort zone might lead to a harsh reality check eventually. Continual recognition and active engagement with one's fears is a distinguishing trait, setting you apart and fueling your journey of consistent advancement.

You Always Need People

Navigating fears and challenges can sometimes feel insurmountable when faced alone. At such junctures, the value of supportive relationships cannot be overstated. These bonds, however, are not automatic; they are cultivated through mutual respect and inclusion in shared growth. The way you engage with and treat those around you serves as an indicator of the support you can expect in times of need, especially during moments of uncertainty or apprehension. Thankfully, a pivotal experience early in my life enlightened me about the importance of such relationships.

In my freshman year of college, my father reached retirement, prompting me to secure employment to aid my family financially. An opportunity presented itself at the electricity board where my father had formerly worked—a contract to paint electricity poles in silver across several districts. While balancing college, I embraced this contract. The stipulated remuneration was Rs 130 per pole, but I was responsible for procuring materials and assembling a workforce. After careful calculation, I hired individuals, ensuring a fair distribution of the earnings post-expenses.

This venture proved to be an invaluable learning experience. It instilled in me the art of resource procurement, team management, and the intricacies of generating profit. Together, as a cohesive unit, my team and I embarked on this venture, paving the way for mutual financial benefits.

In the particular region I worked, I was tasked with painting around 1000 poles. After accounting for all expenses and wages, my profit margin stood at Rs. 50 to 60 per pole. For two consecutive years, this venture was my initial brush with personal success. However, just as I was beginning to savor this achievement, tragedy struck.

A deeply unfortunate incident occurred when one of the workers from my team tragically fell from a pole and lost his life. In the immediate aftermath, a crowd assembled, pointing fingers at me for the accident. The times were such that there was no established compensation policy or framework for contract workers. Despite my inner turmoil and uncertainty about managing such a crisis, I decided not to flee the scene. The situation compelled me to confront the worker's grieving family personally. This confrontation made me internalize a profound truth: when you are genuine and kind to people, it is reciprocated. Maybe that was the deep-seated belief that gave me the courage to face the crowd, I pondered.

Reflecting on the two years of the painting contract, I realized that I had fostered strong bonds with my team and, on occasions, even their families. We shared meals at their homes, and our interactions transcended mere professional exchanges. I never placed myself on a pedestal; rather, I embraced an egalitarian approach, valuing and respecting their contributions. It's imperative to remember that every job is an exchange of skills for money, and just as their skills were invaluable, so was my investment. This mutual respect fortified our relationship.

So, in the wake of the tragic incident, when I approached the deceased worker's family to convey my condolences, their response was unexpected. Recognizing the genuine concern and respect I had consistently shown them, the family, as well as other team members, stood up in my defense against the aggrieved crowd. They acknowledged the event as a tragic accident and emphasized that the deceased had slipped unintentionally. This poignant episode underscored a significant lesson for me: acts of kindness and respect, when extended to others, come back manifold, especially during crises. A foundation of trust and mutual respect not only nurtures strong bonds but also helps navigate challenging situations.

This revelation came to me at a pivotal time, right as I was on the cusp of completing my graduation. Bolstered by the confidence stemming from my previous endeavors, I transitioned into the healthcare sector, an area I was deeply passionate about. While my academic credentials did not support a direct path to becoming a doctor, I remained undeterred and heeded my inner voice, which compelled me to venture into healthcare in some capacity.

My quest led me to a Diagnostic Center in Hyderabad, which, at that time, boasted the only CT scanner in the entire state of United Andhra Pradesh. I secured a position as a ward boy, the only role available to me then, assisting technicians in developing X-ray and CT scan films in a darkroom.

The modest monthly salary of 600 rupees didn't dissuade me. Rather, my unbridled passion fueled my rapid career progression. Within three years, I was helming the center as its manager. This managerial stint acted as a springboard, propelling me to establish my own diagnostic center subsequently.

By this point, I was not just a professional but also a family man, with a loving wife and a daughter. Yet, as my roles expanded, a new set of apprehensions began to gnaw at me. The responsibilities of being a provider, a husband, and a father weighed heavy, and the apprehension of potential adversities at my center loomed large.

While professionally I was soaring, personally, I felt I was veering off course, becoming too engrossed in my work, and drifting away from the very essence of life I had envisioned. Despite my financial stability, a sense of contentment eluded me. My nightly reflections became dominated by these concerns, prompting introspection and a desperate search for solutions.

It was during one of these contemplative moments that I acknowledged my journey's trajectory—from an entry-level ward boy to a diagnostic center owner. Despite my success, I sensed the need for change, for further growth. This led me to seek out Dr. Sangitha Reddy, the then CEO of Deccan Hospitals Corporation and the fourth daughter of Dr. Prathap Chandra Reddy, the esteemed founder-chairman of the Apollo Group. With my wife's assistance, I penned a letter to Dr. Reddy, detailing my experience and expressing my desire for a consultation regarding potential opportunities. This pivotal meeting not only assuaged my concerns but also catalyzed a transformative phase in my life and career.

In retrospect, Dr. Reddy emerges as a guiding force in my healthcare journey, playing the role of a mentor par excellence. Yet, it would be naive to assume that this was the end of my challenges. Life, by nature, is a tumultuous blend of apprehensions and setbacks. The key lies in confronting these fears, leveraging the opportunities that come our way. Opportunities do not cease; they are omnipresent, awaiting those who earnestly seek them. It's imperative to seize them, face our fears head-on, and occasionally, take calculated risks. With each conquered fear, we evolve, and this evolution marks our personal growth journey.

2
EMBRACING FAILURE: A PATH TO GROWTH

Fear and failure share a profound connection. For many, the mere anticipation of failure instills a deep-rooted fear, preventing them from taking proactive measures. Conversely, there are those who develop this fear as a direct consequence of encountering failure. In both scenarios, this fear can significantly erode an individual's self-assurance and impede their path to success. Essentially, if one doesn't fixate on the possibility of failure, the fear of taking positive action is eliminated. Historical figures exemplify this mindset. Swami Vivekananda from recent history and Lord Sri Rama from the Ramayana are prime examples of individuals who, despite facing challenges, never let fear or the possibility of failure deter them.

Everyone Fails!

In the Ramayana, from a unique vantage point, one could argue that Lord Rama faced a series of setbacks, each testing his resolve and resilience. Upon the brink of his coronation, destiny shifted, and he found himself exiled into the wilderness for fourteen years. Yet, Rama, undeterred by this sudden turn of events, didn't wallow in self-pity or question his father King Dasaratha's abrupt decision. Perhaps drawing from prior experiences in the wilderness, he might've seen this as an opportunity for further spiritual growth, learning from the sages and seers of the forest.

However, the trials didn't cease there. His beloved wife, Sita, was abducted by the demon-king Ravana, forcing Rama to ally with the Vanaras and wage a war against a formidable enemy. Even upon his triumphant return to Ayodhya and his long-awaited ascension to the throne, he faced yet another poignant personal sacrifice – the exile of his pregnant wife, Sita, to uphold the moral expectations of his subjects.

At every juncture, Rama faced profound challenges. Still, he transcended them all, not by sheer luck, but due to his unwavering commitment to Dharma, the ethical and moral code of the era. While modern sensibilities might question some of Rama's decisions, he consistently adhered to the Dharma, ensuring he remained righteous despite the tribulations.

It is these very trials, his grace under pressure, and his unwavering adherence to principles that elevate Rama from mere royalty to divinity. The ubiquitous temples dedicated to him across the nation are a testament to this reverence. Despite his royal lineage, Rama's humility and approachability endeared him to all, be it prince or pauper. Reflecting on the hardships he endured - from the unforgiving wilderness to the heartbreak of separation from his family - one can surmise that Rama's journey, though filled with setbacks, was a testament to human resilience, moral fortitude, and an undying commitment to righteousness.

Drawing inspiration from the Ramayana, one can glean that facing adversity without preemptive fear can yield rewarding experiences. When confronted with the idea of forest exile, many of us might crumble under the weight of our apprehensions. Thoughts like, "What dangers lie ahead? Will I or my loved ones fall prey to wild beasts or demons?" would cloud our minds, preventing us from seeing any potential benefits. Yet, with a positive outlook and unwavering resolve, such challenges can transform into opportunities for growth, much like Rama's exile. He cherished the serene beauty of nature, the invaluable time spent with his loved ones, and the wisdom gleaned from the sages of the forest. To him, this exile was not a punishment but an enriching experience, far removed from the confines of palace life.

Diving deep into epics like the Ramayana, Mahabharata, the Bhagavad Gita, Upanishads, and even contemporary philosophy and literature, one can find a treasure trove of lessons on resilience and overcoming fear. Reading these stories with an eye on practical applicability, I've discerned that challenges and failures are an intrinsic part of life. But rather than viewing them as insurmountable hurdles, I see them as opportunities for personal growth. Failures, in my opinion, act as a vaccine, bolstering our resilience against future setbacks. I've had my fair share of failures early in life, but with introspection and the right attitude, they became steppingstones to success. Recognizing and learning from failures illuminates the path forward, leading us to greater heights and brighter futures.

Don't Be a Moustache Baby!

Each setback I've encountered has paved the way for greater endeavors, challenging me to reach new heights. Such a perspective can be nurtured only when one is observant of their surroundings and introspective about their actions and reactions. Literature, particularly Indian literature and philosophy can be instrumental in honing these faculties. When an individual delves into and truly understands these texts, they can incorporate their teachings into daily life. Merely reading the Bhagavad Gita without implementing its wisdom is a hollow exercise. These ancient texts encompass invaluable life and management lessons. From the Ramayana to the Upanishads, if one studies their authentic interpretations, the teachings penned down by the Rishis overflow with profound wisdom aimed at guiding humanity. While Amar Chitra Kathas might serve as an introduction to these tales during our younger years, sticking solely to these simplified renditions stunts intellectual and spiritual growth. Failing to progress from these basic versions to the in-depth insights provided by the Rishis means one remains in a perpetual state of naivety, reminiscent of what Swami Vivekananda described as "moustache babies." The distinction between knowledge and wisdom is crucial.

Often, it is hesitation, a manifestation of fear, that stands between us and potential success. It's this reluctance that delineates those who ascend in life from those who remain stagnant. Those who act without hesitancy often emerge as influential leaders, while others, plagued by inertia, apprehension, or an outright dread of failure, constantly delay decisions. It's not uncommon to hear people attribute their inaction to a lack of cooperation from others. But without taking that initial step, one can't definitively say whether support will be forthcoming or not. This pattern of negative forecasting leads many to cocoon themselves in a supposed 'comfort zone,' resistant to any change. Consequently, many remain trapped in their roles, with a housekeeper continuing in the same position for years or a ward boy spending his entire career without seeking growth.

In retracing the trajectory of my life, my aspirations of becoming a doctor persisted even after the initial stumble in the 10th grade. Determined to join the medical fraternity, I aimed to crack the medical entrance after my intermediate. The next chapter of this journey took me to Guntur, where I convinced my father to finance my coaching and accommodation. Each day revolved around rigorous preparation. But alas, destiny had other plans, and I missed the mark yet again.

This second setback was more pronounced than the first. With whispers of my repeated failures and perceived squandering of my father's resources, my self-belief took a massive hit. Accepting my situation, I shifted gears and pursued a regular undergraduate course. Concurrently, I seized an opportunity to work as a contractor for the electricity board. This new avenue reignited my confidence and reinforced my resilience. Upon graduation, my compass once again pointed towards healthcare. What began as a humble journey as a ward boy soon changed as I defied the stereotypical trajectory associated with that role.

Reiterating my earlier point, fears and failures are not dead-ends but rather pivotal moments that offer enlightenment and growth. My life stands testament to this belief. Despite the inadequacies of my academic journey and the absence of a plush job post-graduation, my early skirmishes with challenges rendered me better equipped to navigate future adversities.

Engaging in battle with one's fears and pushing past failures is a deliberate choice. There will always be phases where exhaustion and doubt threaten to halt your progress, making it easy to succumb and miss out on transformative opportunities. Reflecting upon my own journey, I can recall moments where I hesitated or held back, waiting for someone else to take the lead, which resulted in missed opportunities. Each of these instances underscores the importance of proactive engagement in shaping one's destiny.

During the formative years of my career in marketing, I had the chance to be mentored by a consultant. Our interactions, however, were marred by her abrasive and often disparaging approach. As time wore on, I found myself increasingly uncomfortable in her presence. Negative thoughts began to germinate in my mind: "Perhaps I could sidestep these sessions. They don't seem very beneficial anyway." These thoughts marked the onset of avoidance, a strategy that, in the absence of a backup plan, usually spells self-sabotage.

In retrospect, I now see the dual opportunities I let slip through my fingers due to my hesitancy. The first was the chance to gain valuable knowledge. I could have addressed the discord I felt with the consultant, negotiating a more conducive learning environment. Alternatively, I could have sought other avenues to assimilate the information she was imparting.

The second missed chance was even more profound - an opportunity for leadership. By diplomatically confronting her, not only could I have rectified our personal dynamic, but I could also have championed the well-being of my peers, potentially cementing my position as a promising leader in the process.

After a few instances of such missed chances, I took a moment to introspect and recalibrate. I realized the importance of being proactive rather than passively waiting for external changes. My new mantra became: "Before responding to the outside world, first confront and counsel oneself." By centering oneself and focusing on internal introspection rather than external factors, you're often better positioned to make informed and optimal choices.

Be Proactive!

After much reflection on the myriad opportunities that came my way while managing my diagnostic center, I found myself on the precipice of a pivotal moment in my career. As touched upon in the inaugural chapter, I yearned for the next big leap in my journey. Guided by my wife's sage advice, I penned a letter to Dr. Sangitha Reddy, detailing my professional journey and requesting an audience to present a proposal for her esteemed organization.

To my elation, Dr. Sangitha Reddy responded positively, granting me a month-long opportunity to familiarize myself with the workings of every department in the hospital. This immersive experience allowed me to gauge the hospital's potential and strategize marketing initiatives that could spur its growth. A month later, with a well-laid-out plan in hand, I approached Dr. Sangitha Reddy, whose faith in my vision led her to entrust me with the role of Assistant Manager in Marketing, with a starting monthly remuneration of Rs. 3600/-.

Thus began an exhilarating chapter both for me and for private healthcare in India. In an era when private hospitals were still striving for acceptance, the audacious goal of expanding the prestigious Apollo Hospitals brand across the nation seemed near-herculean. Yet, for someone like me, time was merely a construct. I believed that constantly watching the clock was counterproductive. True progress was achieved by focusing on the task at hand, unburdened by the passing hours. This ethos, coupled with innovative outreach programs, catapulted me to the esteemed position I hold today.

At the heart of this meteoric rise was the unwavering support of my wife. Her belief in my capabilities and her undying faith in our shared dreams bolstered my resolve at every juncture. Much of my success can be attributed to her steadfast presence. In the ensuing chapters, I will delve deeper into her invaluable contributions and the instrumental role she played in my life.

Create and Innovate!

Innovation holds paramount importance in one's trajectory towards growth. It's about discerning the existing chasm between the demand of the masses and the supply you or your organization can offer. Bridging this gap innovatively is the secret sauce to success, a sentiment echoed by numerous accomplished entrepreneurs. This principle, while universal, can be applied effectively across any profession or organization.

During my tenure in Apollo Group's marketing department, I identified one such chasm in the form of medical insurance, which was a relatively nascent concept at the time. I recognized that people usually remembered the importance of medical insurance primarily during medical emergencies. Leveraging this insight, we spearheaded a marketing campaign which reaped considerable benefits. As a result, I garnered recognition and accolades both internally and externally, which played a pivotal role in advancing my career.

By capitalizing on such opportunities, we not only further our personal ambitions but also contribute meaningfully to society and our organization. Such contributions rarely go unnoticed. In my own journey, my relentless efforts in the realm of marketing were acknowledged by the hospital management, which culminated in a series of promotions. From overseeing a small hospital, I progressively rose through the ranks - serving as operations head, vice president of operations, the hospital's COO, and subsequently its CEO.

Today, I proudly hold the title of Regional CEO, overseeing 10 premier hospitals across the Telugu states. Although this journey was peppered with milestones of success, it wasn't devoid of obstacles and failures. Yet, with every challenge I encountered, I took a moment to reflect and identify novel opportunities and charted a forward path with renewed vigor.

The foundational principle I've always upheld is discerning the overarching needs of the broader community or society and aligning one's ambitions and passions to address those needs. Crafting products or programs that resonate with and aid the masses epitomize authentic and sustainable growth. Authentic growth is invariably intertwined with the betterment and prosperity of the community around you.

A quintessential takeaway from this is the understanding that by fostering growth within your community and making a positive difference in the lives of those around you, you inherently foster your own growth. If you catalyze community advancement, that community, in gratitude and acknowledgment, will elevate you.

A poignant photogravure of this ethos is Dr. PC Reddy Garu, the esteemed Chairman of the Apollo Group. As the pioneering visionary behind India's contemporary healthcare landscape, he has ascended to global renown in the healthcare sector. Dr. Reddy was fueled by the ambition of affording Indians access to world-class healthcare right at home.

Today, under his leadership, Apollo Group not only serves Indians but also attracts international patients seeking quality healthcare. Despite these monumental achievements, Dr. Reddy remains remarkably grounded. He perceives every Apollo employee as an extension of his own family, often saying, "Whatever I can do for my family, I should be able to do for you as well." His open-door policy allows even the most junior employees to voice their concerns or offer feedback directly to him.

It's noteworthy that numerous significant improvements within the hospital have been realized due to these transparent interactions.

Such an attitude, one of humility and inclusivity, propels individual growth.

However, there lies an inherent flaw in seeking growth in isolation. If your aspirations are solely centered around your individual success, sidelining the collective good of your community or society, it's a short-sighted endeavor. Pursuing individualistic goals at the expense of societal welfare will inevitably culminate in failure, for you remain a part of that very society you neglected.

3
NURTURING POSITIVITY: HELPING YOURSELF AND THE SOCIETY

Inherently, we are born with a disposition towards optimism. Yet, as we navigate the journey of life, many of us absorb, inherit, or adopt negative beliefs and fears. Therefore, cultivating a positive mindset becomes crucial not only to shed these unfounded apprehensions but also to triumph over the inevitable setbacks we encounter.

Yes, You can!

Throughout the initial chapters, we delved deep into the concepts of fears and failures as that is predominantly where our personal odysseys commence. Each one of us invariably encounters these challenges. Yet, their true essence lies not in their inevitability but in their potential to catalyze change.

They form the bedrock upon which the edifice of our success stands tall. Drawing further on that analogy, think of a Positive Mindset as the foundational pillar reinforcing that structure. As touched upon earlier, opportunities to transcend one's fears and setbacks are always around, if only one is vigilant enough to spot them.

But seizing these chances and propelling oneself forward requires an unwavering belief, a voice within that constantly echoes, "Yes, you can."

The genesis and mechanics of a pessimistic mindset have been elaborately detailed in our prior discussions. Now, embarking on the journey towards fostering a positive mindset commences with acknowledging and embracing your fears and failures. Denying or evading your intrinsic truths only sets you up for recurrent confrontations with them. To truly liberate oneself, one must critically analyze these negative sentiments, follow them to their logical conclusions through astute introspection, and in doing so, eliminate their lingering shadows. This process is the essence of mental alchemy.

The human psyche is intricate, with layers upon layers of thoughts, emotions, and patterns that define how we interpret and interact with the world around us. The story of the well-learned guru and the individual in search of power aptly illustrates this complexity.

In our daily lives, we are constantly bombarded with a myriad of thoughts and instructions, both explicit and implicit. The guru's directive, "Do not think of a monkey," might seem simple at the surface, but it entices the mind to wrestle with the exact idea it's being asked to avoid.

Our minds have a proclivity to focus on the forbidden or the prohibited, precisely because they present a challenge.

This anecdote can be likened to the phenomenon of "ironic process theory" in psychology, where deliberate attempts to suppress certain thoughts make them even more salient. Think of the adage, "Don't think of a pink elephant." The very act of trying not to envision a pink elephant inevitably brings its vivid image to the forefront of one's mind.

Negative thoughts, fears, and insecurities act in much the same way. They're those persistent monkeys, clinging to our backs, refusing to let go. No matter how fervently we attempt to shake them off, they latch on even tighter, their grip strengthened with every denial.

But it's essential to understand that banishing these thoughts isn't about brute force or sheer willpower. It's about introspection, acceptance, and a methodical process of understanding their origin. It's about treating these thoughts as external observers, dissecting them without judgment or bias. This detachment allows us to discern their root causes and address them with clarity.

Much like the individual in the story, we often search for external solutions – be it mantras, rituals, or even tangible objects – believing they hold the power to transform our lives. In reality, the key to personal growth and transformation lies within. It's in understanding that to truly free ourselves from the relentless monkeys of negative thoughts, we need to confront them head-on, understand their nature, and only then can we hope to set ourselves free.

Take Positivity from Anywhere and Everywhere

The inherent duality of life means that there exists both light and shadow, positive and negative, in nearly every situation and character. This is a truth that permeates history, literature, and our daily experiences. Recognizing and understanding this duality is a testament to one's maturity and wisdom.

Consider the broad spectrum of human experiences. Failures, setbacks, and even outright tragedies can harbor lessons and catalysts for growth, should we choose to seek them out. A holistic approach to life, one where we consider both the positives and negatives of any situation, provides a richer and more nuanced understanding of the world.

Drawing parallels with sports is apt. In every defeat, there are lessons to be learned, strategies to be adjusted, and resilience to be built. Conversely, in every victory, there lies the risk of complacency. The defeated party might analyze their shortcomings and come back stronger, while the victor might rest on their laurels. Thus, it becomes essential to glean positive insights from both victories and defeats.

The epic of Ramayana offers a timeless tale of duality. While Ravana is predominantly painted with the brush of villainy, a deeper dive into his character reveals facets of wisdom, strength, and governance. Lanka, under his reign, flourished and was a beacon of prosperity. His knowledge spanned various disciplines, and he was an ardent devotee of Lord Shiva. These qualities stand in stark contrast to his arrogance, lust, and eventual downfall. However, they offer a broader understanding of his character and the nuances that define him.

Our perspective and our lens of viewing the world, plays a pivotal role in shaping our experiences. We have the power to choose our focus. By dwelling solely on negativity, we risk being consumed by it. Alternatively, by acknowledging the negative but choosing to focus on the positive, we foster a mindset of growth, resilience, and optimism.

Cultivating such a mindset is, indeed, a form of meditation—a daily practice of introspection, reflection, and conscious choice. It's a journey of training the mind to sift through the myriad experiences of life and to hold onto what propels us forward, enriches our understanding, and contributes to our growth. In this relentless pursuit of positivity, we not only uplift ourselves but also contribute to making the world a brighter place.

Intrinsic motivation and self-direction are the cornerstones of maintaining a positive outlook on life. There isn't a one-size-fits-all formula or a predetermined set of steps to achieve positivity. It's a deeply personal journey, rooted in individual commitment, discipline, and the conscious decision to view the world through a lens of optimism.

Starting each day with a pledge to oneself—to embrace positivity, to seek joy in the mundane, to extend kindness, and to approach tasks with enthusiasm—lays the foundation for a resilient and optimistic mindset. Just as we nourish our bodies with balanced meals, it is essential to feed our minds with positive affirmations, setting the tone for the day ahead.

At the heart of human existence is an innate desire for hope and positivity. These are the driving forces that push us forward during challenging times, anchor us during storms, and inspire tales of triumph over adversity. While external circumstances play a role in shaping our experiences, it's our internal compass—our mindset—that ultimately determines our reactions and our resilience.

There are countless stories of individuals who, against all odds, have transformed their challenges into steppingstones, leveraging their struggles as learning experiences. What differentiates them from others is not the absence of obstacles but their approach towards them. Their undying spirit and unyielding positivity become their guiding light, leading them to success.

To sum up, while the world around us is ever-changing, and life is replete with unforeseen challenges, the power to cultivate and maintain a positive mindset lies within us. Embracing this power, reaffirming it daily, and using it as a beacon can make all the difference in our journey through life.

Peace Comes with Positivity, and Growth Follows Peace

Life is a tapestry of experiences, emotions, and thoughts, both positive and negative. Understandably, it's human nature to react to adverse circumstances or betrayals with feelings of resentment, anger, or sadness.

These reactions are instinctive and often arise from a deep-seated desire to protect oneself. But while these feelings are natural and valid, lingering on them can create an internal battleground, making peace and happiness elusive.

Our minds are powerful tools, and the thoughts we entertain, both consciously and subconsciously, shape our reality. Negative thoughts act like anchors, weighing us down and preventing us from moving forward. It's essential to recognize that these feelings, while real and valid, are transient. Holding onto them creates a mental fog that obscures our ability to see situations clearly and objectively.

On the other hand, embracing positivity and forgiveness is not about denying our feelings or being naive. It's about taking control of our mental space and choosing peace over turmoil. When we opt to forgive, we aren't necessarily condoning the actions or words of another.

Instead, we're freeing ourselves from the chains of resentment and anger, allowing our minds to focus on growth, understanding, and healing.

Choosing to view situations from an objective perspective, as challenging as it may be, enables us to approach problems with maturity and clarity. It provides us with a vantage point that is not clouded by raw emotions but illuminated by understanding and empathy. This perspective doesn't just benefit us but also those around us, fostering an environment of harmony and mutual respect.

In conclusion, while it's impossible to control all external events, we can control our reactions to them. Choosing positivity and objectivity over negativity allows us to navigate life's challenges with grace, ensuring our personal growth and well-being. It's a choice that paves the way for a fulfilling and peaceful existence.

Life's journey is interspersed with moments of clarity and confusion, happiness and sorrow, hope and despair. Amidst this ebb and flow, the mind's propensity to latch onto negativity can overshadow the beauty and potential of the present. As the influential thinker Jiddu Krishnamurti rightly pointed out, our anxieties about the future often rob us of our present contentment. We tend to magnify challenges or uncertainties looming in the horizon, even before they manifest, leading to unnecessary distress.

Imagine you're on a serene drive through a picturesque landscape, but instead of taking in the immediate beauty, your focus is on an upcoming turn or potential roadblock miles ahead. This mindset doesn't just deprive you of the joy of the moment but can also make you prone to mishaps because you're not entirely engaged in the present. Such is the case with life. By constantly ruminating on what might happen in the future, we miss out on the simple pleasures and opportunities that today offers.

The art of living in the present is akin to unwrapping a gift. Each moment is a present, brimming with experiences, lessons, and emotions. If we're always fretting about the future or dwelling on the past, we fail to unwrap and appreciate this gift. It's important to acknowledge that life's uncertainties are inevitable. However, how we approach these uncertainties makes a world of difference. By cultivating a positive mindset and grounding ourselves in the present, we become better equipped to handle challenges, build meaningful relationships, and enjoy life's many blessings.

In essence, living in the now is about being fully immersed in each moment, appreciating its uniqueness, and trusting that the future will unfold as it should. Such a perspective doesn't just enrich our personal experiences but also fosters communities where optimism, unity, and resilience thrive.

Striking a balance between planning for the future and being consumed by its uncertainties is an art. While it's natural and even necessary to think about what lies ahead, getting entangled in the web of incessant worries can cripple our ability to function in the present. As touched upon earlier, the key is to approach future concerns with a mindset of problem-solving rather than fear. If there's something actionable to be done, do it. If not, incessant fretting will only drain our energies, often about situations we cannot control.

Yet, the cycle of negative thinking persists for many because the practice of positive thinking is, indeed, a learned skill, requiring diligent effort and repetition.

Furthermore, the essence of human existence lies in our interconnectedness. Our successes and failures are not just personal milestones; they ripple out, influencing the larger community. Progress that excludes or marginalizes parts of the community is neither sustainable nor truly successful. True growth and development are inclusive, lifting everyone as it rises.

It's essential to remember that society, as an entity, isn't inherently against any individual. Personal conflicts may arise with individuals within the community, but projecting those individual conflicts onto the entirety of society is misguided. In our interactions and endeavors, the paradigm should shift from an individualistic "I" perspective to a collective "we." This is not just an altruistic approach, but a practical one. By fostering a sense of community, we cultivate an environment where everyone thrives.

Understanding and internalizing this collective mindset requires introspection and a clear sense of one's values. When this inner clarity is established, minor conflicts or negative encounters with individuals become easier to navigate. Recognizing that malice or unkindness is often a sign of another's insecurity or emotional turmoil allows one to approach such situations with compassion rather than aggression. And as history has shown, enduring change and progress are achieved through peaceful means, not violence. Violence, after all, is a manifestation of impotence and desperation. The truly strong find solutions in unity and understanding, always championing the path of positivity.

Positivity is The Nutrition for Your Mind!

Indeed, the interplay between the mind and body is a profound one, and this relationship significantly impacts our overall well-being. Just as we curate the food we eat, being discerning about the information and stimuli we expose our minds to is paramount. In this era of digital saturation, where we're inundated with a deluge of data daily, sifting through and absorbing what's beneficial while discarding the redundant or harmful is essential.

The body's intricate system, with its myriad of enzymes and chemicals, responds not only to the physical nourishment we provide but also to our emotional and mental states. Anxieties, stress, and other negative mental conditions can lead to tangible physiological changes, exacerbating health issues or manifesting new ones. A stressed mind can elevate cortisol levels, a hormone linked to various health complications when persistently high.

As we navigate this rapidly evolving world, the nature and definition of mental well-being also transform. What constituted a balanced and progressive mindset a few decades ago may not be wholly applicable today. With shifting societal norms, technological advancements, and changing global challenges, the mental tools and strategies we employ to maintain positivity and balance have to be updated. It's akin to updating the software on a device to ensure it operates efficiently in a changing digital environment.

However, while the specifics of maintaining a healthy mind may vary across generations, the foundational principles remain consistent. The importance of discernment, the cultivation of positive habits, the nurturing of healthy relationships, and the pursuit of purposeful goals are timeless tenets. As we journey through this dynamic world, recognizing the symbiotic relationship between our mental and physical health and prioritizing both is the cornerstone of holistic well-being.

Absolutely, the landscape of challenges and opportunities has dramatically shifted over the years. While the past generations grappled with the scarcity of basic amenities and resources, our present era comes up with its own set of unique challenges, primarily in the form of information overload. While we have an unprecedented access to information, the onus is on us to discern the valuable from the frivolous.

In earlier times, wisdom was often passed down through oral traditions and experiential learnings, preserved by elders and shared within communities. Venturing into nature or embarking on spiritual pilgrimages were avenues for seeking enlightenment and deeper insights.

Today, the woods of wisdom might be metaphorically represented by the vast digital forests of the internet, libraries, and academic institutions. Yet, the essence of the quest remains the same: the pursuit of knowledge, understanding, and enlightenment.

Indeed, with the democratization of information, we're empowered to question, challenge, and form our own opinions. This is both a privilege and a responsibility. Just as in the past, the wisdom of elders served as guiding lights, today, amidst the cacophony of digital voices and opinions, seeking genuine wisdom becomes even more crucial.

Identifying trustworthy sources, understanding the difference between knowledge and wisdom, and recognizing the timeless principles that underpin a meaningful life are essential skills in this era. While we have countless tools and resources at our disposal, the journey of cultivating wisdom is an internal one, rooted in self-awareness, critical thinking, and an unending curiosity about the world around us.

The role of mentors, gurus, or guides remains as significant today as it was in the past. Their experience and insights can provide invaluable perspective. Yet, in an age of diverse voices, it's also crucial to hone our inner compass, ensuring that we remain grounded in values and principles that resonate with our core beliefs and aspirations.

Give Back to Society!

Every individual holds unique value because they've been endowed with distinctive capabilities and potential. It's believed that these talents are a divine gift, intended to uplift not only the individual but also their community. The journey to recognizing this innate ability often involves exploration, reflection, and understanding how one can serve both personal and communal goals.

When one acknowledges and hones their intrinsic skills, they can become a beacon of positivity and change in society. However, self-awareness without grounding can lead to hubris. It's imperative to identify and nurture this unique passion or skill, mastering it not just for personal gain, but also for the betterment of society.

We thrive in a structured society, enjoying myriad benefits that are the results of countless generations' contributions. This society affords us security, education, knowledge, and opportunities. Expressing gratitude and contributing back is not just a kind gesture but a responsibility.

If we closely observe, nature too operates on a cycle of reciprocity. The mutual exchange of oxygen and carbon dioxide between humans and plants or the cyclic relationship between our consumption and the nutrients returned to the earth is testament to this symbiotic relationship. Similarly, societal growth relies on a continuous cycle of give and take. If we disrupt this balance with excessive self-interest, we jeopardize the future stability and prosperity of society and subsequent generations.

Cultivating a positive mindset and understanding of societal interconnectedness is essential, and this education begins at home. Instilling these values in our children is our duty. But more than mere words, it's our actions that leave a lasting imprint. Children emulate what they see. If we hope to foster a future generation that champions positivity and societal growth, we must first embody these principles ourselves. It's in refining our actions and beliefs that we pave the way for a brighter, more harmonious future.

Drawing from the pages of the Ramayana, we still celebrate Lord Rama not for any supernatural feats but for his unwavering positivity amidst overwhelmingly negative circumstances. Unlike Lord Krishna, who is often depicted with mystical powers, Rama's divinity lies not in magical displays but in his character and perspective. The adage, "Ramo, Vigrahavan Dharmah," reverberates this sentiment, suggesting Rama is the embodiment of Dharma or righteousness.

To personify virtue, one must understand and enact their dharma with unwavering positivity. Our roles shift fluidly throughout our lives — we are sons and daughters, siblings, spouses, parents, friends, employees, and citizens. Each role comes with its unique set of duties. A prevailing issue in today's fast-paced world is our inability to remain present. While with a spouse, the mind wanders to friends; amidst friends, thoughts drift to familial obligations. This scattered focus muddles responsibilities and can lead to internal discord.

Recognizing the distinct responsibilities each role holds and maintaining a positive, present focus while fulfilling them is paramount. This clear discernment and dedication not only streamline one's life but also ensure one's narrative is aligned with righteousness.

4
THE POWER OF SELF-REFLECTION: DISCOVERING YOUR TRUE POTENTIAL

Self-reflection stands as a cornerstone for growth, both for individuals and organizations. This introspective practice offers a gateway to understanding our fears, failures, and propelling us towards positivity. It marks the inception of one's journey towards personal evolution, regardless of life's stage.

Engaging in introspection allows us to scrutinize our thoughts and actions, delve into our apprehensions and missteps, and subsequently chart a positive trajectory. Beyond merely navigating past fears and failures, self-reflection ignites the flame of possibility. Without this inward questioning, our mental growth remains stunted, stifling innovation and creativity. Only through groundbreaking endeavors can one truly taste success, and self-reflection is the catalyst that fuels such extraordinary pursuits.

My moment of Reflection!

Self-reflection plays a pivotal role in fostering innovation. In the early stages of my career at Apollo, the institution had garnered a reputation for being a high-cost hospital. At the time, India's healthcare landscape was dominated by nursing homes, with a distinct absence of corporate or private hospitals offering critical care. Individuals often found themselves waiting for surgeries at government hospitals, and for severe illnesses or complications, they sought treatment abroad. Apollo emerged as a beacon, serving as a corporate hospital aiming to bridge this healthcare gap. It provided top-tier specialty treatments on par with international standards.

However, this innovative approach was unfamiliar to the average Indian. Due to its comparative expense against General Hospitals and Nursing Homes, Apollo often appeared inaccessible. This perception led to financial difficulties, as we struggled to appeal to the broader populace. This was the backdrop some 30 years ago when I took on the role of assistant manager in Apollo's marketing division. As a senior member of the team, the onus was on me to address this challenge and craft a viable solution.

Amidst the mounting pressures to augment hospital revenues and management's ambitious plans to establish a chain of hospitals, I took a different route. Instead of diving headfirst into expansive strategies, I opted for a more reflective approach. I prioritized understanding our immediate environment, gauging the ground realities, and pinpointing potential opportunities. This focus on local insights, stemming from self-reflection, became instrumental in reshaping our marketing strategies.

One day, I stood near the emergency department of my hospital, and keenly observed our patients and their families, hoping to glean insights into their immediate needs. At that moment, I happened to witness an extremely emotional scenario. An auto-rickshaw hurriedly pulled up, and out stepped a middle-class couple with their eight-year-old daughter, whose leg appeared to be fractured, presumably from a minor mishap. The mother, without hesitation, carried her daughter into the emergency room. Meanwhile, the father settled the fare with the auto-rickshaw driver.

Inside, I watched as the mother began to take off her bangles and jewelry, placing them on the counter, imploring the attending physician to quickly attend to her injured daughter. The depth of a mother's love was evident in her willingness to part with her valuables without a second thought.

Contrastingly, when I stepped outside, I observed the father in a heated exchange with the auto-rickshaw driver over an extra charge of 50 paisa. The stark contrast between the two parents' reactions struck me deeply. Here was the mother, ready to relinquish her valuables in a heartbeat for her child's well-being, and on the other hand, the father, fighting ardently over a seemingly trivial amount. Both parents, in their own ways, were doing what they believed was best. The father, likely the sole breadwinner, was ensuring every penny was accounted for, while the mother's singular focus was the immediate care of their daughter.

A short time later, as the young girl's treatment continued, I approached the father who was waiting outside. I inquired about his heated disagreement with the auto driver, especially given the current circumstances with his child. He responded, "Sir, my life is a daily battle to earn. By sheer luck, my elder daughter is soon to be wed. But now, with this accident, I'm anxious about the bill from this corporate hospital. If I exhaust all my savings here, how will I fund my elder daughter's wedding? I must be cautious with every penny."

His words shed light on the myriad perspectives at play: the father's financial concerns, the mother's urgency for their child's health, and the hospital's challenge to provide quality healthcare yet remain financially sustainable. I found myself in the unique position to potentially address all these concerns. It was a defining moment for me. I was driven to make quality healthcare at Apollo accessible to those who felt it was beyond their reach.

Back in my office, I reflected deeply. How could I bridge the gap between the needs of patients like this family and the hospital's mission? The dilemma kept me awake that night, grappling with my role and responsibilities. "Have I chosen a career in healthcare merely to turn away those who struggle financially?" I pondered.

By dawn, clarity emerged. The hospital's intent was noble: to offer top-tier medical care to Indians, eliminating their need to seek treatment abroad at much higher costs. The challenge was to strike a balance between quality care and affordability, especially in an era when quality healthcare was a rarity domestically.

Having settled my thoughts, I turned my focus to the predicament faced by the mother and father. She prioritized her child's immediate health, while he was weighed down by unforeseen medical costs. The solution seemed evident – an affordable accident insurance scheme tailored for middle-class families to address unexpected emergencies. This would not only assist individuals but also ensure a steady inflow for the hospital.

Eager to set this plan in motion, I consulted with our management team and connected with insurance providers to explore creating this new scheme. To my surprise, I learned that such an accident insurance plan already existed, but public awareness was severely lacking.

How then, could we make this scheme known in a way that resonated with the public? Recalling the poignant incident with the young girl, we devised a campaign titled, 'Chotu's Accident Shouldn't Stop Didi's Marriage' (The Young One's Accident Shouldn't Halt the Elder Sister's Wedding). Another powerful slogan we crafted was, 'Physical Accidents Can Lead to Fiscal Accidents.' Consequently, we launched a product named 'Dhosth' – which translates to 'friend,' epitomizing the adage, 'a friend in need is a friend indeed.'

Under the Dhosth initiative, we offered accident insurance at a mere 100 rupees per month. This provided coverage of up to Rs. 50,000 at that period's value. Apollo pledged not to retain any part of this insurance money, ensuring that the entire amount went toward the patient's treatment in the event of an accident. We also introduced disability insurance, which granted a compensation of one lakh rupees to anyone rendered disabled due to an accident.

During that period, the Dhosth insurance initiative became a potent instrument for Hyderabad's residents and gradually permeated other Indian cities. I further extended this momentum by launching a school program. This approach informed children about the scheme, and through these young ambassadors, their parents also became aware. Consequently, many families opted for insurance coverage for their children. This venture marked a significant milestone in both my career and Apollo Group's growth trajectory, benefiting numerous families. The success of this initiative earned me multiple national awards and accolades from the then Chief Minister of Andhra Pradesh.

This entire journey stemmed from a moment of introspection and acute awareness of my surroundings. This experience affirmed my belief: without self-reflection, innovation remains elusive. My creative solution emerged when I began to deeply question my actions and motives. Was I on the right path? Did I have the appropriate product? Was I serving the greater good or merely benefiting my organization and myself? Only after navigating through these pivotal questions was I able to devise an offering that truly benefited all stakeholders. As I've always maintained, when you understand and address a community's needs from within, you inherently make the right decisions.

For me, the objectives were lucid: foster a successful framework for Apollo Group within India, provide better financial safety nets for individuals, and continue my professional ascent. These were my guiding lights. From this juncture, I adopted a habit of continually reevaluating my actions against my goals. Before committing to any endeavor, I asked myself: Is this the right step? Is it aligning with my broader vision? It underscored an essential lesson – the necessity of introspection before defining one's objectives.

Reflect Before You Set Your Goals

Genuine self-reflection is pivotal before delineating one's goals. When I embarked on my career, my sole ambition was to contribute to the healthcare sector. The ascent to becoming a CEO was gradual and not initially foreseen. However, I always yearned to make a meaningful difference in society through healthcare. Starting as a ward boy, the most foundational role in the industry, I recalibrated my objectives, reflecting on my circumstances and seizing opportunities. At times, I was proactive in carving out these opportunities, understanding that they won't always conveniently present themselves.

Before committing to a goal, it's imperative to grasp its underlying "why" and map out the requisite steps towards realization. Unfortunately, many overlook this introspective phase, leading to unmet aspirations. The absence of preliminary self-reflection often undermines the journey towards one's goals.

Recognizing one's strengths, passions, and motivations for a particular objective is crucial. While some narratives claim we can achieve anything, it's essential to understand that excellence in everything isn't feasible. Every individual has a unique purpose in life. When discovered, it can propel one to unparalleled expertise in that domain. This sense of purpose becomes clear when we engage in introspection and self-awareness.

Conducting a personal SWOT analysis – evaluating one's Strengths, Weaknesses, Opportunities, and Threats – is a potent tool for self-awareness. It's a common misconception that SWOT analyses are reserved exclusively for companies or products. Yet, each individual stands to benefit from this introspective exercise.

Whenever I interact with people, I often inquire about their personal business plans. This question typically catches them off guard, as the idea of an individual having a 'business plan' seems unconventional. However, unless you chart a clear roadmap for yourself, how can you expect to contribute meaningfully to your organization, advance in your career, or experience personal growth?

Begin by delving into your own SWOT analysis, distinct from that of your company's. Understand your inherent strengths and how they can propel you forward. As you envision your growth, prioritize the prosperity of the community or organization you are part of.

As I've stressed in previous discussions, when you nurture the growth of your surrounding community or company, your personal ascent inevitably follows. Conversely, if you're driven solely by self-centered ambitions, disregarding the collective growth, you might find yourself on the path to disappointment.

When your strengths contribute to the betterment of your company and society, it initiates a symbiotic cycle. This creates a value chain where those around you support and fuel your growth in reciprocity. Therefore, your personal growth should align with the progress of your company and community. Clearly define how your strengths can benefit both your immediate environment and the broader society.

Acknowledging your weaknesses demands sincere introspection. Identify the areas where you might unintentionally hamper your progress, or that of your company and community. You can either mitigate these weaknesses or strive to transform them into strengths. It's vital to harness your strengths and mitigate your weaknesses in service to the collective advancement. Your strengths often pave the way for opportunities, whereas your weaknesses, if unchecked, can pose threats. These opportunities or threats may manifest through individuals, circumstances, or technology. For instance, if continuous learning is a strength of yours, then rapidly advancing technology could present numerous opportunities. Conversely, if you lag behind in knowledge compared to well-informed peers, this disparity could pose a threat. Overcoming these challenges is crucial to achieving your goals.

After this introspective exercise, you'll be better positioned to identify and leverage suitable opportunities. It's essential to be discerning and not jump at every chance that appears. Evaluate how each opportunity aligns with both your personal and organizational objectives. Embrace only those opportunities that fit seamlessly into your strategic plan, leaving yourself open to future opportunities more in tune with your aspirations.

Promoting Self-Reflection!

From an early age, children should be introduced to the concept of self-reflection. This principle ought to be woven into our education system and parenting ethos. We often err by guiding our children towards courses or careers merely based on their perceived financial prospects. Instead, when our children stand at the crossroads of education or career decisions, we should empower them to make choices informed by their individual SWOT analyses rather than societal pressures or expectations. By engaging with them in this process, we foster a deeper understanding of their unique strengths, weaknesses, opportunities, and threats, and abstain from imposing our personal aspirations onto them. As they progress in their education and life, this self-awareness becomes an invaluable tool, equipping them to navigate various life stages and challenges.

This self-understanding ensures that when they seek employment or affiliation with an organization, they choose one aligned with their intrinsic strengths and passions. Often, people falter by hastily accepting any available job without prior introspection. As they settle into these roles, responsibilities mount—both personal and professional. Eventually, they might feel trapped or unsatisfied, realizing that their chosen path doesn't resonate with their core passions or strengths. Even if they achieve expertise or outperform peers in such roles, the inherent motivation might be missing, hindering their ability to contribute meaningfully to their organization, community, or society.

Being engaged in a career that aligns with one's passion and strengths fosters a genuine appreciation for and desire to contribute to the surrounding community and society. On the contrary, a misalignment can be deemed a failure, not just professionally, but also in the broader sense of not serving oneself, family, company, community, and society. Much of today's societal tumult can be attributed to this mismatch.

Thus, it's imperative to guide our young graduates to conscientiously select careers that resonate with their true passions and strengths. A society filled with individuals operating from their zones of passion and strength will invariably thrive. Remember, the world is brimming with opportunities, especially when approached with a clear, young mind.

Discovering opportunities aligned with your SWOT sets you on a trajectory for success and personal growth. As you enhance your strengths and address your weaknesses, you will naturally encounter more opportunities and fewer threats. Yet, it's crucial to recognize your unique strengths and choose an organization that resonates with your values, rather than making decisions based on external pressures.

Upon completing my degree, I too grappled with the perplexing decision of choosing the right career path. Through self-reflection and a SWOT analysis, I discerned my passion for healthcare and realized my strength lay in engaging with people, a testament to my desire to make a positive societal impact. However, my degree didn't directly correlate with healthcare, making it a less evident choice for a career path.

During this period, my father, a retired state government employee, secured a position for me at the Hyderabad Mint Compound, a Currency Printing Press under the Central government. Thanks to his connection with the Mint's General Manager, who was once his tuition student, I had an opportunity to join a stable government job with a promising future. Yet, I declined the offer.

My vision didn't align with the Mint Compound's work, sparking considerable disagreement with my father. Even as I began my career in the healthcare sector as a ward boy, and later secured a marketing role at Apollo, my father couldn't fathom why I'd forsake a stable government job for what he deemed as less prestigious roles.

It took seven years, and the success of my 'Dhosth' initiative, for my father's perspective to change. An article about the initiative, featuring an interview and photograph of mine, provided the turning point.

After reading that piece, my father's displeasure transformed into pride. He recalled the conversation, gifting me his cherished old pen—a possession I still treasure.

"After reading your interview, I grasped the depth of your passion. I now comprehend why you declined the government job. I'm immensely proud of the impact you've made on society and how you've bettered many lives through your initiative," he conveyed. His words, validating my years-long career choice after an extended period of disapproval, marked one of the most rewarding moments in my life—seeing my father take pride in my accomplishments.

Your Value System!

Undertaking a SWOT analysis not only provides insight into one's capabilities and challenges but also illuminates an individual's core value system. This intrinsic set of beliefs primarily stems from the familial surroundings of one's youth. Primarily, parents and, to a lesser extent, mentors play a pivotal role in shaping this system. It's during the formative years that the foundation of values is laid, making it a crucial period for parents and educators to guide children.

They must not only impart lessons and narratives about values but also exemplify them in action, allowing children to organically assimilate this system into their psyche. This ingrained value system later serves as a compass when one is choosing opportunities or organizations that resonate with their foundational beliefs.

An illustrative example of the profound influence of one's value system is seen in the life of Apollo's esteemed Chairman, Dr. Prathap C Reddy Garu. Hailing from an affluent background and enjoying a thriving career as a cardiologist in the US, he could have comfortably continued in that path.

However, driven by the value system instilled in him, he heeded the call of his father, who urged him to return to India and contribute to its healthcare landscape.

Holding onto the letter his father wrote, Dr. Prathap C. Reddy left his established practice in the US and returned to India, starting with a modest clinic. This endeavor eventually blossomed into the Apollo Group, India's pioneering corporate chain of hospitals. Today, Apollo stands as not only a significant contributor to India's GDP but also as a beacon of healthcare excellence, touching countless lives both within India and beyond its borders.

Be Honest to Yourself!

Reflecting on your actions, understanding the needs of those around you, and discerning how you can address them is a vital exercise many of us neglect. As I mentioned in the initial chapter, it's essential to engage in self-reflection at the end of each day. Dedicate 10 to 15 minutes to introspect on the day's events, evaluating which actions resonated with your core beliefs and identifying any missteps. This self-assessment demands utmost honesty; deceiving oneself is one of the most detrimental habits one can cultivate.

Recognizing and admitting one's mistakes is integral to personal growth. When you identify a wrong committed during the day, not only should you endeavor to improve the following day but also rectify the mistake and, if necessary, apologize to the aggrieved party. If one finds this challenging, it's indicative of a flaw in their value system. Apologizing and moving forward harmoniously underscores the importance of honesty and integrity. As I've emphasized earlier, life is a cycle of actions and reactions. These personal transactions, driven by honesty and responsibility, inevitably circle back to you.

Regular self-reflection serves as a purifying process, alleviating daily stresses and tensions. Ignoring or denying one's misdeeds only embeds a persistent undercurrent of guilt. Over time, these unresolved feelings can accumulate, weighing heavily on one's conscience and well-being. However, through consistent self-reflection, one can expel such negative sentiments daily, fostering a mental environment conducive to both personal well-being and growth.

Revisiting the Ramayana, there's an instructive episode about Hanuman's mission to Lanka in search of Sita. After flying a vast distance across the ocean and battling numerous demons, Hanuman scoured Lanka but found no trace of Sita. Frustrated and despondent, he perched atop a tree, wrestling with the grim prospect of returning to Rama empty-handed. He pondered the heart-wrenching impact such news would have on Rama, how Lakshmana might react, and the broader consequences for Ayodhya and its allies. Momentarily, like many who face seemingly insurmountable challenges, Hanuman contemplated ending his life.

However, the monkey god's strength of character shone through as he paused and reflected: "Have I truly exhausted every avenue in my quest for Sita? Did I explore every corner?" He recalled mistakenly intruding upon Ravana's chambers, spotting some disrobed women. At first, he chastised himself for the perceived misstep. But upon deeper introspection, he realized his intentions had been pure; he sought Sita everywhere, without exceptions. He questioned whether he had overlooked any locations and resolved that taking his own life wasn't the answer. He needed to ensure he had left no stone unturned in his search. Bolstered by his self-reflection, Hanuman persisted and eventually found Sita in the AshokVan.

This story underscores the profound importance of self-reflection. Regular introspection enables us to evaluate our actions, discern right from wrong, and take corrective measures when necessary. A positive mindset is crucial in this journey. Dwelling on negativity impedes progress and can be self-destructive. To achieve success and true contentment, we must consistently shed negative thoughts and reinforce our positivity. In this endeavor, self-reflection emerges as an invaluable ally, guiding us along the right path.

5
CULTIVATING RESILIENCE: BOUNCING BACK FROM SETBACKS

Resilience and positivity are two intertwined virtues pivotal for one's journey to success. While positivity is the beacon that illuminates our path through fears and failures, resilience is the driving force that propels us to surmount new challenges that consistently emerge. It's inevitable: no matter your level of expertise or brilliance, setbacks will appear in various chapters of your life. The capacity to rebound each time and redirect oneself towards success is fortified by unwavering positivity in the face of adversity. To use a mathematical analogy, resilience could be visualized as the cumulative integration of undeterred positivity across varied circumstances.

Resilience revolves around adjusting one's mindset in the aftermath of challenging scenarios, enabling a persistent positive stance, and thereby facilitating optimal decision-making even under strain. Growth is often born from such decisions. As previously highlighted, challenges serve as gateways to opportunities that gauge our mettle. Encountering challenges or failures is, in essence, an essential education. They not only help us comprehend adversity but also prime us for more robust resilience in subsequent encounters. The heightened resilience empowers us to navigate these challenges, make constructive choices to mitigate their impacts, and soldier on.

Thus, the defining line between success and failure is often drawn by resilience. Both the triumphant and the defeated encounter obstacles; however, the successful individual perceives them as learning experiences and nurtures resilience to excel even when the going gets tough. True success demands preparation, both mentally and physically, to elevate oneself to newer horizons. Conversely, those who view challenges as insurmountable roadblocks often halt their journey and deviate elsewhere. Only the relentless drive of a resilient individual can breach barriers or unveil opportunities in any domain.

Keeping at it!

Starting my career at a Diagnostic Lab in Hyderabad was a humble beginning after my graduation. Back then, my daily commute involved pedaling my father's timeworn bicycle. By that point in my life, I'd already weathered numerous failures and challenges. Yet these past setbacks, rather than deterring me, had endowed me with the resilience to stay positive and tenacious. My innate passion for medicine and healthcare served as my guiding light. Initially, my primary role was assisting technicians in developing X-ray films and CT scans. Nevertheless, my enthusiasm led me to invest additional time learning about CT scans, understanding how they aid physicians in diagnosing ailments. This proactive learning approach soon had me wear the hat of a technician, a progression noticed and rewarded by our management.

However, I didn't want to stagnate there; I envisioned a broader horizon for myself. To further my growth, I actively sought collaborations with hospitals and doctors, particularly neurologists and surgeons who often rely on CT scans for diagnosis. Unlike the conventional 9 to 5 workday followed in diagnostic labs, with their mandated breaks and weekends off, I chose to offer round-the-clock services. My commitment was unwavering: anytime a doctor reached out, irrespective of the hour, I promptly provided the necessary scans. I was acutely aware of the ripple effect in the healthcare system: my swift response could expedite patient care, aiding not just the physicians but also the individuals in distress.

Doctors not only began directing more patients to our diagnostic center but also didn't hesitate to call me during the wee hours, trusting my commitment to emergencies. One memorable incident involves a doctor from Nizam's Institute of Medical Sciences (NIMS) reaching out to me at one in the morning concerning a critical head injury case. He was hopeful for an immediate scan that could potentially save the patient's life. Without a moment's hesitation, I was on the job. Due to my thorough knowledge of diagnostics, I was able to relay and interpret the scan results to the doctor over the phone. Such urgent interventions often made the difference between life and death.

This proactive and collaborative approach with medical professionals solidified my reputation within the city's healthcare community. Despite being a technician by designation, my name began resonating amongst healthcare professionals, especially within the doctor fraternity.

Recognizing my continuous drive, the management offered me a role in marketing. My increased interactions with doctors and hospitals in this new capacity paid off, and within three years, I was appointed the manager of the diagnostic center. Eventually, I embarked on my entrepreneurial journey by launching my own diagnostic center. Later, I joined Apollo Group's marketing team, steadily climbing the ranks from an entry-level position to the echelons of leadership.

My ascent in the healthcare sector was largely due to my unwavering passion and resilience amidst diverse challenges. Resilience is indispensable for success. Regardless of one's background, resilience equips you to confront and overcome distinct challenges. Just as we cannot appreciate light without darkness, the sweetness of success is truly understood only when juxtaposed against the bitter experiences of failures and setbacks.

Past Experiences Always Help!

Upon joining Apollo group's marketing team, I began to develop innovative ideas that benefited both the organization and the patients. My progressive approach and effective strategies led to my promotion as the hospital in-charge. During this period, numerous challenges came my way, but one incident stands apart due to its gravity and emotional impact.

A grievous error occurred when two deceased bodies - one male and one female - were mistakenly swapped. Both bodies, completely covered, were sent to their respective families located at distant places. The error came to light when one of the families unveiled the body to find a male instead of their departed daughter. Tragically, by the time they reached back to the hospital, the other body had already been cremated. The anguish of the family was immeasurable; not only had they lost their daughter, but they had also been deprived of a chance for a proper goodbye.

Being the hospital in-charge, the responsibility to address and resolve this devastating error fell upon me. News of the mishap quickly spread, leading to an angry mob gathering outside the aggrieved family's residence. As I approached the situation, a whirlwind of emotions and thoughts consumed me: "Why am I in this situation? I didn't personally cause this mistake, so why do I need to face the consequences?" Yet, an inner voice reminded me of the potential this situation held for my professional growth. Additionally, my previous encounters in challenging circumstances and my inherent empathetic nature prepared me to handle this delicate situation.

I met with the grieving family, addressing each member personally - the father, the mother, and other close relatives. I laid out the truth transparently, ensuring they understood it was a genuine error. Being a father, I felt their pain deeply, recognizing the profound grief they must have been experiencing. My approach wasn't limited to a one-time interaction. Over the next few days, I continuously reached out, offering any assistance or service to somehow alleviate their pain. My persistence, humility, and resilience helped navigate this heartbreaking situation, making it an indelible experience in my career journey.

Dealing with Stress!
Embracing challenges can indeed be stressful, but such stress can be instrumental in our growth. It is stress that metamorphoses coal into diamonds. Without stress, we risk stagnation, and it's only through confronting stress that we discover our full potential. However, it's essential to cultivate strategies to manage stress and to persevere despite hurdles.

Many people turn to yoga or meditation upon recommendation, hoping for an immediate reprieve from stress. While these practices can be effective, sporadic sessions often fail to provide lasting relief. Dipping into them for a few days and then returning to a stress-filled routine without any coping mechanisms is counterproductive.

From personal experience, I've found that indulging in hobbies outside of your professional sphere is therapeutic, particularly in high-stress environments. This could be stress from work, family, or social engagements. A parallel passion – be it for music, sports, literature, or any other pursuit – can serve as an effective anchor, recentering you amidst chaos.

Everyone has their own sanctuary. It could be meditation, yoga, a religious or spiritual ritual, physical activity, travel, or reading. These self-chosen refuges act as our stress-relievers.

The world offers an abundance of experiences beyond our primary profession, so it's beneficial to engage in activities that resonate with our heart.

For me, music and reading have been my mainstay. Having been trained in Carnatic music for nearly a decade, and having performed and released albums in my younger days, I now sing purely for personal solace. Additionally, my spiritual conversations with what I consider my inner self, or God, ground me.

This intrinsic dialogue, whether about mundane or complex topics, keeps me spiritually aligned. Traveling, especially to historical temples, is another avenue through which I reconnect.

Yet, above all, I fervently believe in the power of reading. Not only does it introduce us to diverse worldviews, but it also fosters patience, resilience, and understanding. Recognizing that our struggles are not unique and that challenges are universal is enlightening. Books provide invaluable insights into the human experience and remain an accessible tool for life's teachings.

Strength of Discipline!

Life demands discipline. Reflecting on the disciplined ways of our parents and grandparents, we might question their restrained approach to life. Yet, it's evident that our enhanced lives today are a testament to their disciplined choices. The journey of humanity from primal existence in forests to a refined civilization stands as evidence of the power of discipline and maturity. While it's essential to revel in life's pleasures, it's equally crucial to strike a balance. Extreme work can induce stress, but a lack of it breeds lethargy and stagnation. In any endeavor, the significance of discipline cannot be overstated. Consider the Ramayana's antagonist, Ravana. Despite his eventual fall from grace due to his misdeeds, he rose to immense power and respect largely due to his discipline and adherence to Dharma.

Before the grievous error of abducting Sita, Ravana was revered as Lanka's benevolent ruler. Even when Hanuman set Lanka aflame and took the life of Ravana's son, Aksha Kumara, Ravana showed restraint. Heeding Vibhishana's counsel, he refrained from executing Hanuman, a messenger. It was this discipline that fortified Ravana, making it a formidable task for Rama to vanquish him. Thus, discipline is paramount. When adhered to, it carves out ample time for various pursuits and empowers us to navigate challenges adeptly. Challenges are inevitable life phases, not insurmountable barriers.

Even as toddlers, we face the initial challenge of learning to stand and walk, a hurdle we almost universally surmount. As we tread further in life, the complexity of these challenges amplifies. In this context, the importance of nurturing and guidance during one's formative years cannot be emphasized enough.

Let Them Struggle A Bit!

Instilling resilience in our children is essential for their holistic development. While our protective instinct as parents naturally drives us to shield our children from adversity, doing so excessively might rob them of opportunities to grow and fortify themselves. Society, unfortunately, has segments that equate overprotection with affection.

This well-intended, yet misguided, approach can lead to children being ill-equipped to handle stress. Consequently, even minor setbacks might push them to take drastic measures. Hence, it is imperative both as parents and as a society to strike a balance, allowing children to face challenges, with our support as a safety net.

True resilience isn't about constantly battling challenges, but about maintaining inner strength and making judicious decisions in the face of adversity. It demands patience, focus, adaptability, and courage, among other traits. Discernment lies in recognizing which trait to employ at a given moment.

Understanding the healing power of time is key to patience. Throughout life, there will be moments when one contemplates extreme actions. But with patience, many issues dissipate with time. I highlighted this in the first chapter, reflecting on my personal moments of despair after failing matriculation. Even legendary figures like Lord Hanuman had moments of doubt during his quest for Sita. In such moments, patience can pave the way for clarity and better decisions.

Adaptability, too, is a cornerstone of resilience. Nature has a simple rule: those who adapt thrive, while those who resist wither. Darwin's theory of evolution emphasizes the survival of the fittest.

Dinosaurs, despite their dominance, failed to adapt and thus became extinct. In professional settings, adaptability is a linchpin for success. If one resists aligning with an organization's culture, it might hinder growth or even result in expulsion.

Conversely, adapting to the organization's ethos while retaining one's core values can be a catalyst for progression. This adaptability isn't confined to professional spheres; it extends to our personal roles as siblings, parents, and more. I believe in being like water: adaptable in shape without compromising its essence. This philosophy has been a guiding principle in my life.

People Behind My Resilience

Throughout my life, I've been fortunate to be surrounded by resilient individuals who inspired me, many of whom were close family members and colleagues. Leading the list are my parents, who navigated significant financial challenges with grace and determination.

On a modest monthly salary of just Rs.150, my father not only provided for our immediate family of five but also extended his generosity to about 20 other relatives who frequently visited from our village. Despite being the eldest son, he never turned anyone away. His unwavering cheerfulness and understanding of their needs, despite our financial constraints, was a testament to his character.

My mother, in her own right, showcased a different kind of resilience. Despite lacking formal education, she masterfully managed our household on a shoestring budget. More importantly, she instilled in her children the fortitude and ambition to rise above our circumstances and stand tall with dignity. Her quiet strength and indomitable spirit left an indelible mark on me.

Lastly, my wife deserves special mention. At the time of our marriage, I had yet to establish myself financially. But with her steady support, I found the resilience to face numerous challenges head-on.

Holding a Ph.D., she is more academically accomplished than I am, a simple degree holder. In a twist of fate, she was even my superior at work before we tied the knot. Throughout our journey together, I've faced personal, professional, and social setbacks. Yet, she has stood by my side as a pillar of strength, ensuring I never wavered. Her faith in me bolstered my resolve, even in the toughest of times.

Within The Apollo Group, where I have spent a significant portion of my career, two figures stand out for their exemplary resilience and leadership: Dr. Sangeetha Reddy and Dr. Pratap C Reddy.

Dr. Sangeetha Reddy, the Group Managing Director of Apollo, has been my mentor and guiding force. In the fledgling years of Apollo, the company grappled with financial setbacks, making it challenging to even disburse employee salaries. Yet, I personally witnessed Dr. Sangeetha's commitment to ensuring that our salaries were paid promptly on the 30th of each month, come what may. Beyond financial considerations, she delved deep into each issue we faced, offering solutions and guidance. Her unwavering support during those tumultuous times not only bolstered the company but also played an instrumental role in molding me professionally and personally. Reflecting upon those times, I realize the profound impact Mrs. Sangeetha Reddy has had on my journey.

The resilience narrative of The Apollo Group would be incomplete without mentioning our esteemed chairman, Dr. Pratap C Reddy. His journey to establish the group was laden with obstacles. In a time when India's regulatory landscape did not favor the establishment of such a healthcare institution, Dr. Reddy faced myriad challenges. Traditional banks were hesitant to finance this uncharted territory of private advanced healthcare. Consequently, he had to seek support from politicians, promoters, and influential individuals, both in India and globally. His determination and tenacity laid the foundation for what The Apollo Group represents today.

It was during the tenure of Rajiv Gandhi that Dr. Pratap C Reddy finally secured the necessary permissions. This marked the dawn of contemporary healthcare in India. Establishing such a prominent healthcare group required an unimaginable degree of commitment and perseverance over several years. Even after the inauguration of the hospital, there were skeptics who ridiculed the idea, suggesting he turn his "5-star hospital" into a 5-star hotel to turn a profit. Undeterred, Dr. Reddy would often quip that he had created not a 5-star, but a 7-star institution dedicated to serving the society that shaped him. He remained steadfast despite initial setbacks.

Fast forward to the present, and we witness a thriving medical tourism industry with Apollo Hospitals at its helm. Patients from all over the world flock to India, particularly Apollo, for cutting-edge healthcare. Such a transformative shift in the landscape of global healthcare would remain a pipe dream if not for the indomitable spirit of Dr. Pratap C Reddy. Remarkably, even in his 90s, he continues to envision and work towards a future of preventive healthcare for all Indians. Guided by his vision, Apollo Group has established an extensive Prohealth department dedicated to preventive healthcare.

I consider myself fortunate to have been influenced by such figures. Their unwavering positivity and resilience in the face of seemingly insurmountable challenges have been a source of profound learning for me.

Resilience During the COVID Pandemic

I'd like to conclude this chapter with a reflection on a recent, profound experience that tested global resilience: the COVID-19 pandemic. The collective perseverance of humanity during these trying times is a testament to our inherent strength and should serve as an enduring inspiration. It was, without a doubt, the most universally shared challenge in modern history.

For my team and me, entrenched in the healthcare sector, the stakes were even higher. Our responsibility was twofold: care for the influx of patients while ensuring our own safety in an environment where circumstances shifted dramatically on a daily basis.

During the onset of the pandemic, like everyone else, we grappled with the unknown nature of the virus. Yet, our duty was clear: we had to provide unwavering care to our patients while safeguarding our own team.

Understandably, the palpable fear was overwhelming for healthcare workers. Many nurses, hailing from distant regions, felt compelled to return home due to familial pressures. This exodus, right at the heart of the pandemic, further strained our resources as patient numbers surged daily.

As the CEO, my administrative role naturally thrust me into the epicenter of these challenges. However, beyond administration lay the monumental task of galvanizing my staff's spirits, ensuring they reported to the hospital daily, unburdened by fear or trepidation. Simply asking them to put their lives on the line while I remained ensconced in the safety of my home was not leadership. So, I resolved to lead from the front. I stationed myself within the hospital wards, sharing meals and accommodations with my dedicated nurses and doctors.

At the age of 55, if I could immerse myself directly in the line of duty, it emboldened my staff, diminishing their apprehensions. Those early days were fraught with uncertainty. Today, our understanding of COVID-19 has matured, but back then, the global healthcare fraternity grappled in the dark, awaiting a definitive cure or vaccine. Despite the ambiguity, we adhered to evolving protocols and safety guidelines, fully aware that there were no guarantees. Our commitment to healthcare mandated unyielding resilience, both for the patients we served and our own well-being.

True leadership isn't solely about personal pliability; it encompasses fostering resilience within one's team. Monumental achievements are seldom the fruit of individual effort. Tackling immense challenges requires shared fortitude. My parting advice is to draw inspiration, whether from those near or distant, and cultivate the resilience necessary to chart your course to success.

6
MINDFUL LIVING: FINDING BALANCE AND INNER HARMONY

Simply put, mindfulness is the act of being fully present. With our inherent ability to recollect and anticipate, we often dwell in the past or fixate on the future. It's become increasingly challenging to truly inhabit the current moment. This pervasive tendency, although embedded in our society, has made it especially arduous for many to genuinely live in the now.

Embracing the Now!

True fulfillment lies in cherishing each unfolding moment. When lost in thoughts of the past, we tend to gravitate towards its negative facets. More often than not, our minds amplify regrets over past mistakes rather than relishing positive memories. This predisposition not only overshadows past joys but also magnifies anxieties about the future. Such rumination can stifle our ability to engage meaningfully with the present.

Therefore, cultivating a positive outlook and resilience from an early age is paramount. Every individual should recognize that challenges and setbacks are universal experiences. The sooner this is understood, the quicker one can diminish unnecessary worries and center attention on the task at hand. This essence captures the spirit of mindfulness. When embraced, it amplifies efficiency, spurs innovation, boosts productivity, and facilitates societal contributions. It lays the foundation for personal growth and achievement.

Mindfulness ought to be a foundational principle of existence. Humans, with their heightened capacity for mindfulness, have emerged as dominant entities on Earth. This very mindfulness has been instrumental in honing our inventive prowess. As we refine our abilities and continually strive for mastery, we evolve, always setting our sights on the next pinnacle of achievement.

Undeterred Focus on Objectives

At its core, mindfulness is about honing one's focus, directing attention to what truly matters, and minimizing distractions. It involves maintaining a sharp focus on one's goals, letting go of past setbacks, comprehending lessons from past failures, and strategizing for the present. This is the essence of mindfulness. Repeating the same actions and expecting varied outcomes is futile. It's imperative to excise worry from one's mindset. Not only is worry unproductive, but it can also exacerbate situations.

As conscious beings, our foremost task should be to clearly define the purpose behind our actions, or pinpoint the specific skill or profession we aspire to master. For those at the dawn of their journey, determining a clear path or objective can be daunting. This is where tools like the SWOT analysis, which I've elaborated upon in prior chapters, prove invaluable. With well-defined life goals, our choices — be it related to career, job, or affiliations — become more intentional and aligned.

However, even with clear objectives, one must navigate the complex maze of human emotions. These emotions can, at times, overshadow our judgment and actions. Staying true to one's objectives and remaining mindful can be challenging when emotions threaten to cloud clarity.

During my early days at Apollo, I faced a situation that tested my focus on my goals. In the nascent stages of my marketing career there, I found myself reporting to a superior who seemed to view me as competition, or even a potential threat to his position. This perception seeded a palpable tension between us. Given his authority over me, direct confrontation wasn't an option, so I internalized this strife. A reservoir of resentment built up inside me, and it began to manifest as a divergence between my external demeanor and inner turmoil. Consequently, my concentration waned, and my efficiency wavered.

Looking back, I discern that subconsciously, my priority shifted from excelling in my role to finding a way to sideline my boss. Instead of channeling my energy into my responsibilities, I was preoccupied with the idea of how to eclipse him. As time progressed, I recognized the toxicity of this path but felt trapped, unsure of how to extricate myself from this self-inflicted quagmire.

One weekend, during a routine visit to the Ramakrishna Math, an unexpected encounter proved pivotal. While I was there to attend a lecture by Swami Ranganath Ananda, I was approached by a young monk I hadn't previously met. He inquired, seemingly out of the blue, about the apparent distress in my demeanor. Drawn to his presence, I found myself pouring out my internal conflicts. Seeking guidance, I questioned, "How do I break free?"

His words were simple yet profound. "The moment you label someone as an enemy, you inadvertently empower them with the ability to dominate your thoughts and actions," he began. "If you truly believe confrontation is the answer, then address it head-on. If not, refrain from casting anyone in the role of an adversary. When you perceive someone's actions as consistently malicious, it's often a construct of your own mind. Instead, approach relationships, especially in the professional realm, as transactions. A transaction is momentary, holding significance only during its occurrence. Once it's concluded, there's no need to replay it incessantly. Learn to compartmentalize and move forward."

This perspective resonated deeply with me. We continued our conversation under the shade of a tree, and he elaborated on the idea of a transactional approach to life's interactions. This encounter was transformative; it shifted my entire outlook. Subsequently, I no longer viewed my superior through the lens of enmity. Instead, I saw our interactions as a series of transactions within the broader narrative of my career.

The crux of this philosophy is understanding the temporary nature of roles we assume in various spheres of our lives. By visualizing situations as transient transactions, we can adapt seamlessly, donning the appropriate 'mask' for each scenario. With family, be the caring partner or parent. At work, be the diligent employee. With superiors, be the respectful subordinate. The versatility to transition between roles is an invaluable human attribute.

Embracing this perspective and consciously integrating it into one's daily life transforms one's experience. Life doesn't just become harmonious; it blossoms in its true beauty. Productivity soars, and erstwhile perceived adversaries often reveal themselves as allies. This very shift occurred between my boss and me. The man I once viewed as a hurdle later became instrumental in my growth. Ironically, he became a guiding figure, endorsing me for promotions, imparting invaluable training, and mentoring me through various challenges.

This chapter of my life was instructive. It underscored the importance of mastering emotions that obscure clarity and compromise decision-making. If one remains true to their purpose and infuses their work with genuine integrity, it invariably benefits the larger organization, community, and beyond. Seeking immediate rewards for every good deed isn't the way to go. If one's intentions are pure and one's efforts sincere, the universe has a way of reciprocating, albeit sometimes in an unhurried, cyclical manner.

Balancing Emotions

People's reactions and behavior toward you often stem from their circumstances, and as those circumstances evolve, so can their behavior. If we allow resentment to dominate our thoughts, it not only sullies our own mindset but can also breed more negativity, leading to destructive outcomes. Conversely, if we approach others with love and respect, the universe has a way of ensuring that goodwill returns to us. Staying vigilant about this is crucial, as it's all too easy for one's mind to stray, especially under external influences. It's vital to exert conscious effort to maintain focus on one's true objectives and shield decision-making from unproductive emotions.

Maintaining this equilibrium in thought and decision-making requires both awareness and consistency. It's easier to achieve if ingrained early in life. Imparting this wisdom to the next generation is crucial, whether through personal anecdotes or literature. Failing to transform our experiences into valuable lessons for the young is a missed opportunity. While it might be challenging to convey the significance of a balanced mindset to every youngster, the onus lies with us to make the effort. The responsibility rests with us, not them.

Many individuals who act negatively within society often lack proper guidance during their formative years. Sadly, such individuals struggle to positively impact both others and themselves. The consequences of a lack of mindfulness are evident daily, from minor road rage incidents causing unnecessary traffic jams to disruptions at social events over trivial matters. These minor instances pale in comparison to the more severe and violent repercussions of mindlessness reported in the news. By instilling mindfulness and a balanced perspective early on, individuals learn to pursue their desires peacefully, eliminating unnecessary chaos. Inner peace not only enhances productivity but also contributes to one's overall health.

Mindfulness has profound health benefits. Our bodies are intricate chemical systems, heavily influenced by our emotions. When we maintain tranquility in our mind and life, our body functions more optimally. Historical sages, known for their longevity, are testament to this principle. Today, certain yoga practitioners, even at 100 or 125 years of age, remain active and robust. This showcases the interplay between one's mindset and physical well-being. Essentially, our mind governs our body's intricate chemical mechanisms. Think of the mind as the CEO of your body, requiring continuous training and practice to cultivate mindfulness.

Constant agitation or harboring resentment can have significant health repercussions. If we can view conflicts or misunderstandings as mere transactions, letting go of negativity, we pave the way for better health and productivity. Even when we believe the other person is at fault, embracing forgiveness can be a transformative step. Mindfulness emphasizes forgiveness as a means to navigate life without the weight of emotional baggage.

Some might justify their short temper by attributing it to their nature. However, such tendencies often stem from a lack of mindfulness training in their developmental years. This absence of guidance can have ripple effects, impacting not just the individual but also their loved ones and broader community.

Notably, most religions emphasize mindfulness. In Hinduism, for instance, practices like meditation, yoga, Sandhya Vandhan, or chanting the Gayatri Mantra have been instruments that past gurus employed to instill mindfulness. These practices promote balance and harmony in one's life. We must remember that humans, too, are a part of nature, so achieving equilibrium is intrinsic to our well-being. It's essential not to be adversarial with organizations or individuals in our surroundings. Instead, focus on honest, sincere actions while staying attuned to the evolving dynamics around you. Taking things for granted can be a significant oversight.

When Dasarath, seemingly on the brink of crowning Rama, instead commanded him to exile to the forests, Rama accepted the staggering shift without a hint of resentment. Many might have felt their world crumble dramatically, but Rama, a paragon of mindfulness, remained serene. His readiness to leave Ayodhya was mirrored by Sita, but Lakshmana grappled with intense distress. The whole turn of events seemed nonsensical to him. In his anguish, he even suggested to Rama that they defy Dasaratha, hinting at extreme measures. But Rama, ever the voice of reason, reminded him, "How can the bond of fatherhood dissolve in a day, based on a single decree? His intention was to crown me, but unforeseen forces, or 'daiva sankalpa,' altered his decision. Our duty as sons is to stand by him."

Rama's graceful acceptance of such a monumental change offers profound wisdom. Bearing grudges or acting impulsively without understanding the underlying reasons of a situation demonstrates immaturity. True mindfulness means remaining aware of the larger context, leading to more informed and mature decisions. This balanced mental state can nurture both personal and professional growth.

7
EMBRACING CHANGE AND GROWTH: UNLOCKING YOUR POTENTIAL

Across six chapters, we've delved into the essential virtues that pave the way for an individual's success. However, it's vital to understand that even with these virtues fully ingrained—whether it's conquering fears, navigating failures, bolstering positivity, cultivating resilience, or mastering mindfulness—success is not always a certainty. One formidable factor that can shift the tides of fortune is Time. As time marches on, it brings about inevitable changes. The inability to adapt to this ever-evolving landscape can cause even the most prepared individuals to falter and lag behind.

Change is Constant and Inevitable!

From sunrise to sunrise, with each new dawn, you find yourself a day older. Just as the earth rotates and orbits, bringing forth inevitable cycles of day and night, in life too, everything is in a constant state of flux. People evolve, landscapes transform, scenarios shift, technology advances, and with all these, the nature of challenges we face mutates. Over a lifetime, you'll encounter an array of individuals, each bringing their unique perspective and attitude to the table. Every change demands an adaptation from your end, a recalibration without resistance. It's through this relentless evolution that you truly flourish.

Embracing change isn't just pivotal for your professional trajectory; it's also the key to mental equanimity. Resisting the inevitability of change is akin to swimming against a powerful current—exhausting and self-defeating. Recognizing and making peace with the ebb and flow of life's changes keeps you anchored and allows you to navigate the seas of uncertainty with grace and poise.

Peace and growth operate in a symbiotic relationship. Just observe the world around you: regions and countries that have managed to maintain relative peace often experience more substantial growth and prosperity. Conversely, tumultuous regions tend to stagnate. This correlation extends to individuals as well—inner peace provides fertile ground for creativity, innovation, and productivity, paving dual tracks towards progress and success.

Reflecting on our ancestral roots, early humans confronted myriad challenges in the untamed wilderness. Their survival hinged on their unparalleled adaptability. From seeking refuge in treetops to evade predators, to adjusting to the whims of nature, they exemplified resilience in every sense. Millennia later, we find ourselves cushioned by the luxuries of modern civilization. Ironically, this comfort has often dulled our innate adaptability. As the world keeps advancing, rekindling this intrinsic human trait becomes more essential than ever. It's time to embrace change, not as a challenge, but as an opportunity for growth and enlightenment.

Adaptability is an increasing challenge for the contemporary generation. As I previously mentioned, had the dinosaurs adapted to climatic shifts, they might still roam our planet. Their extinction underscores a profound lesson: to both survive and thrive, recognizing and adjusting to change is indispensable.

A pervasive issue is the reluctance some may display towards even minor shifts. At 60, if I were to cling to the patterns of my 30s or 40s, expecting them to persist, I'd be setting myself up for disappointment. As leaders or administrators, we must remain abreast of emerging technologies and transformative approaches, ensuring our teams are equipped and agile enough to adapt. Otherwise, there's always the risk of another entity in our industry outpacing us. It is paramount to instill in our teams a proactive mindset geared towards continuous adaptation and evolution.

Central to cultivating a flexible outlook towards change is perceiving the world in its raw, unvarnished state. The truest, albeit sometimes challenging, lesson is to see the world as it unfolds, acknowledging that change is the only real constant.

In the modern era, the frenetic pace of life leaves little room for introspection, especially among the youth. Their hours are consumed by digital diversions such as video games, YouTube, or Instagram. The valuable time once devoted to enriching activities like outdoor play or reading, which foster a balanced mindset, is rapidly diminishing.

While entertainment has its merits, it's vital to grasp that genuine life enjoyment stems from holistic knowledge and a balanced psyche. Unfortunately, there's no one-size-fits-all formula to achieve this equilibrium, given the uniqueness of each individual's cognitive processes. However, a potential remedy lies in reading and embracing diverse perspectives. Engaging with literature doesn't necessitate marathon reading sessions. Even a few pages a day can sow the seeds of a lasting habit. Over time, many discover that reading not only equips them with a more nuanced worldview but also offers deeper satisfaction than most digital distractions, aiding in cultivating a balanced, mature mindset.

Seeking Wisdom

Cultivating a mature and balanced mindset is pivotal in garnering wisdom and embracing change. Our ancestral teachings, revered gurus, and sacred scriptures offer timeless insights that remain remarkably pertinent today. They lay the foundation for our personal growth and emphasize the importance of adapting to life's ever-shifting realities.

In these ancient scriptures, there is an underlying theme of understanding the nature of reality. For instance, the phrase 'Aham Brahmasmi' posits that one's true essence aligns with the divine, Brahma, and everything else we perceive is a mere mirage.

This is further echoed in the saying 'Branthi Mathram Idam Sarvam,' which elucidates that our perceived reality is a fleeting illusion. These ancient teachings impart a profound lesson: that the world around us is in a state of perpetual flux, and what we often perceive as tangible reality is transient and ever-changing.

Similarly, the Bhagavad Gita, an iconic philosophical treatise, reaffirms this notion. It delineates the eternal nature of the soul, or Athman, which remains impervious to worldly harms and changes. In contrast, our corporeal existence is ephemeral, subject to change at every conceivable scale.

From the subtle aging that happens between dawn and dusk to the broader shifts in our lives, change is an omnipresent force. Comprehending this truth is integral to living a life rooted in understanding and acceptance.

I firmly believe that immersing oneself in the wisdom of texts like the Bhagavad Gita, Ramayana, and the profound revelations of ancient Rishis, can guide us towards a harmonious existence, regardless of the society or community we inhabit. Thus, seeking wisdom through such readings is invaluable.

In my personal journey, the inexorable nature of change became evident early on.

Life's trials, both within my family and personal experiences, were stark reminders. The challenges I faced and the resilience I mustered during my youth underscored an essential truth: to navigate life's complexities, one must evolve and adapt to the circumstances rather than harboring hopes for external changes.

Later, as I embarked on my professional journey, Mrs. Sangeetha Reddy's guidance further reinforced this invaluable lesson, instilling in me the mantra of adaptability and resilience.

Finding Acceptance

Nearly three decades ago, when I first began my journey with Apollo, I grappled with the challenge of blending in with my colleagues. As a newcomer, I constantly felt out of place, as if I were an unwelcome addition to the team. This perception led me to believe that the organizational culture was unwelcoming, and perhaps my peers were unwilling to accept me. Overwhelmed, I sought guidance from Mrs. Sangeeta. Expressing my anxieties, I told her I might be better off elsewhere, given how unaccepted I felt.

Mrs. Sangeeta posed a simple, yet profound question: "You believe they aren't welcoming you. But have you welcomed them?"

Caught off-guard, I was rendered speechless. Requesting a day to reflect, I was granted the time. Without the luxury of modern technology, I turned to my drawing board, meticulously jotting down my experiences. I created a chart analyzing each instance, gauging my reactions and those of my colleagues. To my surprise, I discovered that my coworkers weren't always in the wrong. I realized that had I approached situations with a tad more maturity, creativity, and acceptance, the outcomes might have been different.

The following day, I shared my revelations with Mrs. Sangeetha Reddy, walking her through my hand-drawn analysis of my initial two months. She sagely advised that the cornerstone to professional growth was my ability to adapt to change and embrace the people around me. Her guidance was an invaluable lesson, making me recognize the importance of acceptance from my end. I consider her not only a mentor in my professional endeavors but also a guiding star in my personal life. Without her wisdom, I might never have grasped the significance of being the first to extend the olive branch. Those early charts I drew at Apollo still occupy a treasured spot in my collection, serving as a testament to my evolution and the guidance of a true mentor.

Returning to our main discussion, a common misconception many of us have is the expectation for society to mold itself to us. We frequently lament the fact that we feel "out of place" or "misunderstood." But have we ever paused to consider the inverse? Why not be the one to embrace society with its quirks and challenges and then carve our path within it? In my career, this shift in perspective was transformative. Instead of swimming against the current, I began to flow with it. My interactions became more harmonious once I truly accepted my colleagues and partners. This change in attitude was reciprocated, paving the way for a myriad of new opportunities.

The essence of teamwork is collaboration. Regardless of how revolutionary your ideas might be, they remain just that – ideas – without the support of those around you. If your peers don't see you as one of their own, they might be less inclined to value your input. The initial hurdle isn't about the merit of the idea itself; it's about the collective acceptance of the individual presenting it. When you're perceived as an outsider, even the most groundbreaking concepts can be dismissed or undermined. By building trust and mutual respect, you ensure that your ideas aren't just heard, but are also given the consideration they deserve.

Embracing change and accepting those around you acts as a magnet, drawing more allies to your cause. When you're flanked by a supportive team, the scope of what you can accomplish magnifies exponentially.

On your own, you may scale certain heights, but with the combined energy of your colleagues and community, your ascent can be both swifter and more profound. This collective synergy not only fuels faster attainment of goals but often propels you to successes beyond your wildest aspirations.

Such adaptability and inclusiveness were the cornerstones of my early achievements at Apollo. By immersing myself in their culture and gaining their trust, I cultivated a team that reciprocated my acceptance. The beauty of this camaraderie is that the onus of innovation no longer rests solely on your shoulders. With a myriad of perspectives, the pool of ideas is richer, and creativity flourishes.

As a leader, this presents an enviable position: the privilege of cherry-picking the most promising ideas, refining them, and steering the collective towards shared success. The result? A cohesive team that amplifies each other's strengths and propels the organization to greater heights.

Bad Habits Never Help!

Life's complexities can often seem overwhelming, and in the absence of proper guidance, many succumb to negative coping mechanisms. Instead of confronting challenges directly, it's tempting to resort to habits like smoking or drinking as a form of escapism. But true resilience and peace come from authentic guidance, consistent practice, and nourishing habits such as engaging with enlightening literature.

In my own life, I prioritize consistent self-improvement and seek wisdom through deliberate reading. My literary choices have a purpose; I select texts that have enriched my past, present, and will undoubtedly guide my future. The principle is straightforward: negative habits provide no genuine solace.

This isn't to label every individual who drinks or smokes negatively, but using these as escape routes from life's challenges is detrimental. Resorting to alcohol or cigarettes out of fear, or to numb certain thoughts, might offer a temporary reprieve, but the root issue remains untouched.

Masking your problems doesn't eradicate them; it only postpones the inevitable confrontation and further weakens your mental fortitude. In doing so, you're not only diminishing your capacity to address the issue but also overlooking potential solutions. If you truly seek relaxation post-resolution, then face the challenge first and then decide your path. But remember, alcohol, for all its perceived relaxation benefits, often brings with it additional health burdens.

The most constructive approach is to engage with your problems, not flee from them. When faced with a challenge, confront it mentally, dissect its components, and actively seek solutions. By immersing yourself in the issue and examining its facets, solutions often become evident.

However, if you choose to bury the problem beneath layers of detrimental habits, you'll find no resolution. Embrace challenges, scrutinize them, and pursue solutions. This proactive approach is the optimal strategy for navigating life's myriad complications.

Anticipate, Plan, and Grow!

Maintaining a balanced mindset and adaptability to change sets the foundation for the subsequent crucial step: anticipating change. With a keen understanding of the natural evolution of things, it becomes possible to discern patterns in these changes. This ability to predict shifts becomes an invaluable tool, allowing for optimal preparation.

If you can foresee developments in the coming months or year, you can devise strategies accordingly, making your response more proactive rather than reactive.

This foresight becomes particularly essential in the business world. For those at the helm of businesses or involved in decision-making processes, the capacity to anticipate future market shifts, customer preferences, and industry trends is indispensable.

Formulating business models and strategies based on these predictions ensures that even if only a fraction of your anticipations materializes, your preparation will still set you ahead. Moreover, it's prudent to always have alternative plans—Plan B, C, and even D—to cater to various possible outcomes. Such comprehensive planning ensures that your resources, be it manpower or finances, are well-allocated, maximizing your chances of achieving organizational and personal goals.

However, the significance of preparation and adaptability isn't limited to the professional domain. Personal lives, too, are rife with changes, some expected and others unforeseen. As life progresses and responsibilities mount, the key lies in not being overwhelmed but in being prepared.

Observing the world around us, we see a spectrum: individuals shouldering immense responsibilities with grace and equanimity, and others who feel weighed down by the slightest of burdens. Ultimately, it all boils down to perspective—a mindset of welcoming change and seeking growth within it can make all the difference.

Throughout my life, I've had the privilege of being influenced by many inspirational individuals. However, the most pivotal and dear to me is undoubtedly my wife. Reflecting upon the idea of adapting to change, few scenarios epitomize this more than that of a newlywed woman. In my wife's case, the challenges were further amplified, yet her resilience in managing each transition in our journey together has been nothing short of awe-inspiring.

Before tying the knot, she was not just a colleague but also my superior. She mentored me in marketing, shaping my understanding of the subject as I worked under her guidance. Post our marriage, she seamlessly integrated herself into our traditional joint family—a testament to her adaptive nature.

Despite the myriad responsibilities and shifts in her life, she never let go of her academic aspirations. When we were newlyweds, she only held a basic degree. Yet, with strong determination, she pursued her MA even while expecting our first child. Not stopping there, she went on to complete her MPhil and achieved a Ph.D., all while nurturing our two children. Once she earned her doctorate in record time, she joined the Indian School of Business (ISB) as an editor. Her journey didn't halt there. Over a decade, she metamorphosed into a communications maven, eventually founding her own healthcare venture, Argala, specializing in elderly home care services.

Today, she stands tall, not merely because of her professional achievements but because she navigated every twist and turn with grace and tenacity. Whether it was adjusting to a new family, relocating, transitioning through different life phases, or even adapting to industry dynamics, she orchestrated her path masterfully, always moving forward. Her story is a testament to the wonders one can achieve by embracing change and working diligently within its framework.

Dr.Prathap C. Reddy's vision and anticipation of the healthcare landscape four decades ago is also truly commendable. Reflecting on the inception of the first Apollo medical facility in Jubilee Hills 40 years ago, it's hard to believe that the area was once a forested region. At that time, it was considered remote and distant from the city's heartbeat. Many doubted his decision, with some even ridiculing him for selecting such a location. Fast forward to today, Jubilee Hills has transformed into the city's epicenter. Acquiring property in this bustling hub has become nearly impossible, let alone getting it at a reasonable rate. Dr. Reddy Garu's ability to foresee this urban development and secure land at what now seems like a paltry sum is a testament to his vision. His story, along with others I've encountered in my life, underscores the importance of anticipating change and harnessing it for future growth.

Find and Accept Yourself!

Adapting to change isn't instinctive for many of us. To truly embrace change, the starting point is introspection. Recognizing and accepting oneself with all the flaws, is the cornerstone of this journey. If you're not in tune with yourself, adapting to external changes becomes a daunting challenge. This was a struggle I too faced early in my career.

More often than not, we are our own harshest critics. The challenges that surround us, whether they arise from our environment, peers, or societal pressures, are often magnified by our inability to accept ourselves. The foundational principle is to embrace who you are and recognize that change is a constant in life. This self-awareness and acceptance equip you to better navigate and adapt to shifting circumstances.

When you become adaptive and receptive to change, doors of opportunity swing open. Facing change with bravery and a discerning eye allows you to spot these chances for growth. Remember, there's always a silver lining, even in seemingly dire situations. Think of it as gazing at the night sky, a vast expanse dotted with stars and the luminous moon. Opportunities are akin to these celestial bodies. Sometimes clouds obscure our view, but it doesn't mean the stars have vanished. They're merely hidden from sight temporarily. You must be patient, knowing they're still there, and prepare for the moment they reappear. Similarly, you should strategize for change, ready with multiple plans to pivot when necessary. The objective is to clear the clouds and seize the opportunities that await.

One of the most profound lessons I've learned in life is the importance of staying true to oneself. A personal SWOT analysis is crucial. While it's essential to address your weaknesses, there's immense power in acknowledging and harnessing your strengths.

Suppose you excel as a chef; why not aspire to become an exceptional chef? If carpentry is your calling, embrace it with all your heart and strive to be among the best in the field. It's a mistake to undervalue your innate abilities or view them as inferior to others. Every skill is a gift. If you've been blessed with a talent, it's meant for you to refine and celebrate. The error often lies in underestimating our unique strengths and coveting the abilities of others. Recognizing that everyone has their niche is vital. Your prowess is distinct, as is theirs.

By honing your skills and remaining open to change, you position yourself for success. Resistance to change is futile, as change is inevitable. It's a constant in life. Welcoming change, even anticipating it, allows for growth and evolution. After all, adaptability is the essence of survival and prosperity.

True success, however, is achieved when it's accompanied by inner peace. Striving for your goals with a sense of calm not only enriches the journey but also inspires those around you. History has shown that leaders who lead with peace and compassion leave an indelible mark. Mahatma Gandhi's legacy, for instance, is anchored in his principles of non-violence and truth-seeking. Figures like Adi Shankara, Ramanuja, and Madhva are revered for their peaceful and enlightened leadership. It's a testament to the idea that genuine growth and influence are not derived from arrogance but from a place of serenity and humility.

8
CHARTING YOUR COURSE: SETTING AND ACHIEVING MEANINGFUL GOALS

Since the dawn of civilization, humanity's relentless quest for progress has set us apart from the rest of the animal kingdom. This unique drive, rooted in our aspirations, has propelled us from the primitive recesses of forests to the pinnacles of modern cities and digital realms. Unlike animals, who live primarily in the present, humans are forward-thinking, always seeking, always yearning.

Every great civilization, every groundbreaking invention, and every philosophical thought that has shaped our world has been birthed from an innate human desire: the thirst for knowledge, the zeal to understand the universe's intricate tapestry, and our place within it. The ceaseless churn of our curiosity has led us to uncover the mysteries of science, harness the forces of nature, and bridge the gaps between continents and cultures.

However, the path to progress isn't solely about ambition; it's equally about grounding and mindfulness. In the ancient Sanskrit terms, "disha" and "dasha" beautifully encapsulate this idea. While "disha" emphasizes the importance of direction, of having a clear vision and purpose in life, "dasha" speaks to the state of our mind.

True advancement doesn't come from a restless spirit but from a tranquil heart and a mind that seeks growth without forsaking peace. This balanced synergy of aspiration and serenity is the compass that has, and will continue, to guide the human journey through the epochs of time.

Passion Gives You Power!

At the core of every human soul lies a burning ember of passion. It's an inescapable truth; this instinctual drive manifests in each one of us at some juncture of our journey. However, the real challenge lies not in feeling this passion but in acknowledging and nurturing it. Those who harness this fire, aligning their dreams and aspirations with it, inevitably ascend to unparalleled heights. When passion becomes the compass guiding our pursuits, goals cease to be mere checkpoints; they transform into milestones of a journey fueled by fervor.

Drawing from the tapestry of my life, medicine was the beacon that beckoned me. Though I couldn't don the white coat of a doctor, I never let go of my intrinsic affinity for healthcare. Instead of lamenting the roads not taken, I channeled my passion into creating new paths. From the first tiny dot to the present day's successful life, my trajectory was steered by an undying commitment to my passion. My ascent isn't a testament to my individual endeavors alone but a tribute to the transformative power of passion.

Recognizing and wholeheartedly embracing one's passion is pivotal. Yet, it's often a journey fraught with challenges. The societal pressure, the weight of external expectations, or the allure of material success often eclipse our true desires. Many, unfortunately, drift away from their passion's gravitational pull, leading to a life filled with dissatisfaction and ennui. When individuals are driven by external motivations rather than genuine passion, their actions often become transactional. Over time, this can lead to shortcuts, compromises, and sometimes even ethically questionable decisions.

This phenomenon, when widespread, can engender a society marred by disillusionment and chaos.

Thus, to cultivate a harmonious and fulfilling life and, by extension, a thriving society, it's paramount to align our actions with our passions, anchoring our endeavors in authenticity and purpose.

One of the profound gifts that set humans apart from the myriad species on this planet is the depth of our introspection, our ability to think, reflect, and be guided by our conscience. This unique faculty is especially vital when we stand at the crossroads of life, deciphering the path that will define much of our existence – our career choice. Given the gravity of this decision, it's imperative to be governed by a sense of genuine passion and purpose, rather than fleeting whims or external pressures.

For many, finding this inner compass may not be an immediate revelation. And that's alright. The journey to understanding oneself, assessing strengths and weaknesses through tools like a SWOT analysis, can be a pilgrimage in itself. What's crucial is to allow oneself the time and space to embark on this quest of self-discovery. As important as milestones like academics or jobs may seem, carving out a trajectory aligned with one's true calling should hold paramount significance.

Life is seldom a smooth sail. Challenges, be they personal, financial, or social, will frequently arise, casting shadows of doubt and uncertainty. I, too, wrestled with adversities, faced dilemmas, and grappled with constraints as I navigated the labyrinth of life's decisions. When faced with the alluring stability of a government job, juxtaposed against the seemingly precarious path in healthcare, starting right at the bottom rung, I took a leap of faith. My decision wasn't just a job change; it was a testament to prioritizing passion over security.

Had circumstances been different, maybe I would've trodden a contrasting path, aiming for medical school or a prestigious business institution. But life's unpredictability often becomes its most defining trait. While challenges are a universal constant, with the majority encountering their fair share of struggles, they shouldn't dictate our destiny. What truly shapes our journey is our tenacity to confront these adversities head-on, innovatively working around them, ensuring that our passion remains an unwavering north star.

It's vital to understand that embracing our authentic path doesn't negate or belittle our problems. It simply reinforces the conviction that while problems may be inevitable, surrendering our dreams to them is a choice – one that we don't have to make.

Smart Goals Help Your Cause

Goal setting is akin to charting a course for a ship. Too easy a route, and you miss the adventure. Too challenging, and you risk shipwreck. In my journey, I've found the principle of setting 'SMART' goals - Specific, Measurable, Achievable, Relevant, and Time-bound - to be instrumental. But beyond their SMART characteristics, I've always emphasized another crucial dimension to goals: their ethical and societal impact.

In an interconnected world, our actions ripple outwards, touching lives often beyond our immediate circle. Consequently, every goal we set not only influences our trajectory but also the socio-cultural fabric we inhabit. This implies a profound responsibility: to ensure our aspirations uplift rather than undermine the collective well-being.

True, competition is inevitable. It's the engine that drives progress, innovation, and excellence. But it's essential to distinguish between competition and cutthroat rivalry. A healthy competitive spirit seeks to elevate one's performance, striving for excellence, and respecting peers. It's rooted in the idea that we all can rise together, pushing each other to greater heights. On the other hand, a cutthroat approach, driven by self-centered motives without regard for ethics or societal good, is a recipe for discord.

It's naive to think that actions, even if they are narrowly self-serving, won't have broader repercussions. Harmful practices, unethical behaviors, or any endeavor that undermines societal harmony will, in the long run, foster an environment of mistrust and instability. In such a volatile setting, no one truly wins, for the social fabric becomes frayed, making it vulnerable to greater adversities.

Leaders, especially, bear a greater onus. Their goals and actions serve as templates for many. When leadership is laced with selfish motives, it doesn't just disappoint; it corrupts the very ethos of society, leading to widespread disillusionment and chaos.

Therefore, in crafting our ambitions, the compass should not just point towards personal success but also societal betterment. This holistic approach ensures that as we chase our dreams, we also pave the way for a world that's enriched, harmonious, and inclusive. After all, true success isn't just about personal elevation but also about raising the bar for everyone around.

Keep a Tab on Your Health!

The pursuit of success and ambition often propels us into a relentless race, a race where our health and well-being frequently take a backseat. In this bid to climb ladders and touch skies, we overlook a fundamental truth: the foundation of all success is the health and well-being of the self. For how can one truly revel in the joys of achievements if the vessel – the body – that facilitated those accomplishments is worn out and frail?

Ancient wisdom, such as our Vedas, offers profound insights into this symbiotic relationship between the body, mind, and soul. The saying, *'Deho Devalayo Proktho Jeevo Devo Sanathana,'* elucidates this beautiful philosophy. Likening our body to a temple is an evocative metaphor. Just as we approach a temple with reverence, care, and devotion, so should we approach our own bodies. Just as the temple stands tall, its sanctity maintained with meticulous rituals and practices, our bodies too require nurturing, care, and respect.

Moreover, the importance given to cleanliness, purity, and ritualistic preparations before entering a temple serves as a poignant reminder of how we should approach our own well-being. It is an embodiment of the concept that what is external is also internal; the purity, sanctity, and respect we show to a temple should be mirrored in how we treat our own bodies.

When we start viewing our bodies as sacred abodes for our eternal souls, our perspective towards health and well-being shifts. It's not just about exercising or eating right, but about holistic care that encompasses mental, emotional, and spiritual well-being. This philosophy ingrains in us a sense of responsibility, urging us to respect the sanctity of our bodies, just as we would respect a temple.

While ambition is commendable and achievements laudable, they should never come at the expense of one's health. For what good is success if it doesn't bring about happiness and peace? True happiness and peace stem from a harmonious alignment of a healthy body, calm mind, and nourished soul. Embrace your body as the sacred temple it is, and let this reverence guide you in your pursuits, ensuring that your journey to success is not just prosperous but also wholesome and fulfilling.

Obstacles are a Part of Life!

Life's journey to achieving one's dreams is seldom a straight path. More often than not, it is a winding road, strewn with obstacles and challenges. Each barrier, however, holds within it the potential to be a stepping stone, a learning opportunity that can lead you closer to your aspirations.

My journey began with a desire to cure people's diseases. However, when I couldn't clear the medical entrance, the path I had envisioned for myself seemed blurred. Naysayers were plenty, quick to highlight my perceived inadequacies and question my ambitions. Their words were like relentless waves, attempting to erode my resolve, pushing me away from my dream each time I tried to inch closer.

Declining a seemingly stable government job to begin as a ward boy might have seemed, to many, a step backward. But in my heart, I knew it was a step closer to the world I was so passionate about: healthcare. The criticisms and skepticism of others became background noise as I continued on my journey. The path was not without its battles. Each step brought its own set of challenges. From territorial disputes in Apollo to navigating the complexities of organizational dynamics, the road was rough and often lonely.

However, life, in its essence, is a series of challenges. Every day presents its own set of problems, regardless of one's position or status. Even while sitting at the helm of a prestigious international healthcare organization, challenges are a daily occurrence. But therein lies the beauty of it all: if life were devoid of problems, it would also lack purpose. Challenges exist to be surmounted, and in overcoming them, we not only progress individually but also contribute to the greater good, propelling society and organizations forward.

In every challenge, there is an opportunity to showcase one's skill, to grow, to learn, and to make a difference. After all, we are here not merely to exist but to solve problems, to bring about change, to innovate, and to leave an indelible mark. We have to embrace each challenge, for it is in overcoming them that we truly realize our potential and find our purpose.

In the grand fabric of life, challenges and problems are not just inevitable, but they are also essential. Imagine a life devoid of challenges or problems. Such an existence would not only be mundane but also devoid of purpose and growth. Our very existence, the essence of our being, is intertwined with the problems we face and the solutions we seek. It's this very quest for resolution that keeps the fire of life burning within us.

Problems, in essence, are the heartbeat of our existence. A life without problems is akin to a heart without a beat, alive in name but devoid of the life force. Even in our most peaceful moments, like when we are deep in slumber, our minds construct an alternate reality, a dream world, where we confront and navigate myriad problems. Whether we are awake or asleep, our consciousness oscillates between two worlds, both brimming with challenges, emotions, and experiences. These dual realms serve as a testament to the fact that problems are not just external events we face but are deeply woven into the fabric of our consciousness. The challenge then is not to escape problems but to navigate them with grace, understanding that they are but transient waves in the vast ocean of existence.

While we might grasp the importance of challenges, it's also natural for us to sometimes feel overwhelmed, disheartened, or even on the brink of despair. In such moments, our external environment plays a pivotal role. The company we keep can either anchor us, providing stability and support, or can further pull us into the abyss of negativity.

Our ancient Vedic sages profoundly understood this. The saying, "Satsangatve Nissangatvam, Nissangatve Nirmohatvam, Nirmohatve Nischala Tatvam, Nischala Tatve Jeevan Mukti," underscores the importance of good company. In essence, it conveys that good and true companionship leads to detachment, detachment leads to clarity of mind, clarity leads to an unwavering understanding of reality, and this understanding culminates in liberation.

In simpler terms, the company of truthful and genuine individuals can pave the way for one's personal and spiritual growth. Such company can serve as a lighthouse, guiding us through life's storms and ensuring we stay true to our path. Whether in professional settings like the corporate world or in personal spheres, the influence of Satsang or noble company is profound. Surrounding oneself with positive and motivating individuals can make the difference between thriving and merely surviving.

While problems are the roots of our existence, the company we keep is the compass that guides us through them. Embracing challenges, seeking solutions, and cherishing the company of good souls can lead us to the pinnacle of personal and spiritual growth.

Life, in all its complexities and uncertainties, continuously offers us invaluable lessons. One of the most profound truths that I wish to impress upon my readers is this: Never let fear or the daunting shadow of failure hold you back. Life, after all, is not about never falling, but about rising each time we stumble.

Consider the resilience of a ball. When thrown to the ground, it doesn't just lay there. It rebounds, often soaring even higher than before. This ability to rebound, to recover from setbacks, is what each of us should strive to embody.

And if ever you find your spirit flagging, simply turn to nature for inspiration. Nature is a living attestation to resilience and adaptability. Observe the grass on a well-trodden path. Despite being trampled upon day after day, it doesn't surrender. Given even the slightest respite, it seizes the opportunity to flourish once more. Or think about the dense forests, the ever-flowing rivers, and the towering trees. Each undergoes their share of trials, yet they persevere, ever rejuvenating, always thriving.

Reflect upon indigenous tribes, some of the earliest stewards of our Earth. Against the tides of modernity and countless adversities, they continue to coexist harmoniously with nature, drawing upon its abundance while also preserving its sanctity.

The message here is clear: Opportunities for growth, learning, and resurgence are all around us. But recognizing these opportunities requires a shift in perspective. Instead of viewing problems as insurmountable barriers, see them as challenges waiting to be overcome. In every problem, there's a hidden potential for growth, a latent lesson to be learned.

In my own journey, this perspective has been transformative. Embracing challenges, adapting to them, and ultimately surmounting them has paved my path to evolution. So, I urge you to embrace your challenges, for they are not just problems; they are the doorways to your greatest transformations.

In life, our journey is often shaped by the guiding stars that provide us with direction, support, and inspiration. For me, these guiding lights came in the form of three extraordinary women, each of whom has left an indelible mark on my life and career.

My mother, the first and most formidable force in my life, was a masterclass in resourcefulness, resilience, and empathy. Her ability to navigate the trials of life, to stretch every resource to its utmost limit, and to prioritize needs with precision was nothing short of genius. But what left the most profound impact on me was her negotiation skills.

A mother's unique ability to convince, cajole, and comfort was, to me, the epitome of efficient and compassionate management. She taught me the value of making the best of what we have, of understanding needs versus wants, and of the importance of community and collective growth.

Then there's my wife, an embodiment of strength, wisdom, and grace. Even in our professional life, when the dynamics of power could have overshadowed our relationship, she remained steadfast in her humility and unwavering in her support. Her leadership style is one that empowers, uplifts, and inspires growth. She has taught me that true leaders don't stand alone at the top; they ensure that those they lead rise along with them.

Lastly, Dr. Sangeetha Reddy, the mentor who recognized my potential and harnessed it. Under her guidance, I learned the importance of investing in people, of identifying strengths and cultivating them. She was not just a leader; she was a teacher, a guide, and an exemplar. Her approach to mentorship — a blend of nurturing care and exacting standards — has been instrumental in my professional journey.

Each of these women, in their unique way, has shaped me, molded me, and guided me. Their lessons have been my roadmap, their faith my fuel. I owe them a debt of gratitude that words can scarcely express. To them, and to all who have been a part of my journey, I offer my heartfelt thanks. As I pen down these concluding words, I hope that my story serves as a beacon to others, illuminating the way as these incredible women have done for me.

9
WOMEN AS MIRRORS OF SUCCESS

They say behind every successful man, there is a woman. But I would say behind every successful man, there are women. Do you see the difference? Sometimes, it is not just one woman but an army of women propelling an individual towards success.

When I express admiration for women, it does not diminish the importance of men in any way. Success in life is a journey that requires the support of both men and women. It's the collaborative effort of diverse perspectives and experiences that propels us forward.

As an individual, I'm sure you have your own set of skills that are outstanding. However, you can't deny the fact that you require some support to excel in life and conquer heights, can you? As you grew up, your father likely provided crucial support to help you conquer your fears. Perhaps you found yourself terrified of heights, but your father, recognizing your apprehension, may have enrolled you in a swimming class. This strategic move not only exposed you to heights but also empowered you to overcome your inner fears, paving the way for newfound courage and confidence.

While your father played a vital role in strengthening you physically, your mother undoubtedly contributed to your emotional fortitude and sensibility. Whenever you recounted your school day experiences, your mother was there, encouraging you to share your food with friends and to always treat others with kindness. She instilled in you the values of respect for your teachers and the importance of empathy in your interactions with others. Through her guidance and nurturing, she not only shaped your character but also equipped you with the essential qualities needed to navigate life's challenges with grace and compassion.

Reflecting on the cadence of our daily lives, my mother emerged as a steadfast guide, a sage in the art of nurturing. Her care wasn't just in the big moments but in the everyday details. Both my parents had equally contributed to my growth as an individual. While my father shared a wealth of knowledge with me, my mother instilled kindness and wisdom that continues to shape my perspective and choices in life.

Their combined teachings have created a lasting impact, providing me with a balanced foundation of information and discernment that I carry with me to this day. Her wisdom lay not in grand gestures but in her consistent dedication to ensuring her family's well-being.

I have learned the importance of family and the support system it creates for an individual. Despite lacking formal education, my mother imparted insights about life that became the true foundation of our lives. She equipped us with the strength to stand on our own feet, empowering us to achieve the successes that define who I am today. Yaadevi Sarva Bhutesh Vidyarupen Sansthithaha. Without the blessings of our parents, we don't amount to much in life.

Just like lord Shiva uses his third eye to destroy evil and protect the universe, every mother is granted a third eye, which she uses to safeguard her kids. The multitasking skills of a woman are just outstanding. They can literally do twenty different things at a time.

She might not visibly have a third eye or eighteen hands, but if her child is in trouble, she can defeat a hundred Mahishasuras and burn them down to ashes in a moment. Yaadevi Sarvabhuteshu Shaktirupena samsthitaha;

    My mother supported me while I was going through the worst phase of my life back when I was a little boy. Like any other human being, I, too, had to deal with profound moments of misery in my childhood due to my circumstances. Living in an elite society surrounded by esteemed bureaucrats as neighbors, I found myself in a situation contradictory to children my age attending reputed educational institutes. While they absorbed the standards of well-equipped facilities, my reality was extremely divergent — a tiny government school without basic amenities such as benches, toilets, and even teachers; that's all my family could afford. But my mother taught me to be grateful for what we have.

    In my formative years, I had to fight another tough battle that was silently resting inside me–the inability to communicate in English like my peers – the pain it gave me wasn't something that I could easily ignore. Similar to Hanuman's moment of despair in the Ramayana, when he had to go through a challenging phase, or rather, a depressive phase, after exhaustive attempts to find Sita in Ravana's palace, I, too, found myself in a dark room. I was unable to find a way to be capable of speaking fluent English; it was indeed a dark tunnel. During every academic year, I spent days preparing for the final exams, hoping to get promoted to the next grade. It was no less than a herculean task! I used to finish the year with bare minimum marks.

    However, the people in our society who keep waiting for a chance to embarrass our family would take this as the right opportunity to compare me with their children and make me feel discouraged and insecure. Their laughs and tease used to reverberate in my ears for weeks. In the depths of despair, thoughts of surrendering to the darkness loomed above my head for a while, yet divine intervention came in at the eleventh hour, protecting and preventing me from succumbing to the arms of death.

Amidst all the hiccups, a guardian angel named Ambika, my Upaguru, emerged as my strongest pillar of support. Sent by the almighty as a blessing, she helped me navigate through all the challenges of life. Her encouragement became the driving force that restored my faith in living and empowered me to rebound. Ambika, my Upaguru, not only helped me regain my peace of mind but also blessed me with invaluable lessons on resilience and vision. She sat me down and made me understand that giving up is never the right way to get out of a situation. She taught me the importance of resilience and of patience, just like how my mother does. If it weren't for her, my academic life would have been unfathomably sorrowful. With her support, I learned to understand what was once unseen and to move forward in life with newfound strength. Her influence allowed me to continue my journey and left an indelible mark on those around me. Today, as I reflect on my life's journey, I owe much of my resilience and growth to her. She has always been as influential as my mother.

Influence can come from various directions. It doesn't necessarily have to be your parents alone. It can be anyone you have met or have not met. The world we live in, the nature we are surrounded by, the animals we see on roads, and everything else has the capacity to influence our lives on a daily basis. There are factors that can influence us deeply, be it when making a decision or even choosing not to make a decision. If I were to categorize these influencers, I would call them internal and external influencers. Internal influencers are all about the family, and external ones, as we already spoke about, are all about nature. We all grew up hearing the phrase "give and take." What does that truly mean to you? Is it very transactional, wherein you give something to somebody, and then you expect to get something in return? Apparently, that also describes "give and take." But, in my opinion, it is all about "reciprocation."

If nature is providing you with a lot of life lessons, you are obliged to give something back to nature. It is not just about feeding birds or planting a sapling. You could pass on these life lessons to the people you know and help them experience a transformation in their lives.

Looking into nature, you know for a fact that we breathe in oxygen and exhale carbon dioxide. The plants around us consume this carbon dioxide, convert it back to oxygen, and give it back to us. It is a never-ending cycle. It reminds you to contribute something significant to humankind and the planet.

*Growing up, my father has always been a strong supporter. He used to do every*thing for us even while he himself was struggling to make ends meet. He was the breadwinner of the family, and with his support, we all grew up and were fortunate to receive formal education. However, upon my father's retirement from service, I found myself in the middle of completing my twelfth grade. Knowing our family's financial constraints very well, I decided not to become a burden to anyone. Also, I wanted to make my father proud. He put all his efforts into making life easier for his children, and the least I could do for him was to be a great son by not depending on him financially anymore.

To support myself, I decided to start working. While pursuing my degree, I used to work as a pole painter simultaneously. After completing my education, I transitioned into a role as a ward boy in a diagnostic center, marking the beginning of a new chapter in my professional journey. My parents had already done a lot for me, and it was my turn to treat them well. I worked really hard and slowly climbed the ladder in the direction of growth over a long period of time. When you learn to reciprocate, fortune will slowly come your way. All you have to be is genuine and patient.

As I started to ascend the career ladder with greater ambition, I realized that it was the result of my patience, hard work, willpower, and the support of both my parents, my gurus, and the universe. Never had I ever, even in my dreams, thought that I would become the CEO of a prestigious institution like Apollo. It was Dr. Sangita Reddy who saw the potential in me and offered me this position. She holds the key to the professional chapter of my life, and I owe everything I am today to her guidance and support. She's always been a well-wisher, and I can proudly say that she continues to inspire me even today. Under her mentorship, I discovered the essence of "motherly management," a transformative approach that creates a more productive work environment along with a profound sense of commitment.

Dr. Sangitha seamlessly played the roles of a teacher, philosopher, and the nurturing Maa Annapurna in my life. Her teachings embody the spirit of "Yadevi sarvabhuteshu Sarvakaryeshu sarvada," recognizing the divinity in all beings and emphasizing dedication in every endeavor.

She taught me the importance of humility, drawing parallels to Lord Rama's teachings. Through her wisdom, I learned that embracing humility is the key to unlocking my true pot*ential and achieving success in both personal and professional spheres.*

It is Dr. Sangita who gave me this new life, and I will forever be grateful for what she did. She is a very patient and kind individual who is absolutely compassionate towards every individual she meets. I feel that I'm one of those blessed, truly blessed people to be fortunate enough to have met her.

As soon as I joined Apollo, my life started changing. Every day, I get to meet new people with new stories. I have been able to learn a lot from each one of them, and I have been putting all my efforts into making their lives better in the best way I can.

While I had just joined Apollo, my wife, who was then in a much higher position than I was, had also mentored me so well that I learned how to handle situations in marketing. She's always been the cornerstone of my journey. Choosing to depart from the well-trodden path of a Civil Service career, a choice most of her close friends embraced successfully, she dedicated herself to ensuring my stronghold in society. During the initial days of our marriage, she made numerous sacrifices, compromising on basic amenities. She even had to give up on her jewelry quite a few times in order to support the family.

Throughout the turbulence, she took courageous steps. Her resilience and unshakable belief in my potential have always helped me achieve more in life. She has always been a wonder woman – while going through all the ups and major downs of life; she managed to pursue and complete her post-graduation, MPhil, and Ph.D., adding further layers to her achievements.

I can never stop admiring her indomitable spirit and selflessness. If it wasn't for her, I have no clue where I would be right now. Without her, the heights I have reached would have been insurmountable, making her a significant person in the narrative of my life.

I might not be saying thank you to her every day; however, every morning, I ensure that she feels secure and happy. I have always been a great listener for her. Yaa devi Sarvabhuteshu Budhirupena samsthitah ;

Numerous individuals have been pillars of support throughout my journey, offering faith and genuine friendship. Their strong belief in me became a guiding light, enabling me to navigate the most challenging situations and ultimately shape the person I am today. In their collective presence, I found not just allies but a source of strength that propelled me toward my aspirations.

It is very easy to utter "thank you" and "sorry," but if you don't mean it when you say it, you should ideally refrain from using those words mindlessly. Everybody around us is fighting different battles. All that is expected of us is kindness. Being nice to people doesn't make you any less happy; it only improves the quality of your own life. Apologize if you are wrong and convey your gratitude from the bottom of your heart if they have done something for you.

Now that I have said

about apology and gratitude, let me explain it from an Indic perspective.

In Sanskrit, there are two beautiful words- Kruthagnjya and Kruthagna. "Kruthagnjya" encapsulates profound gratitude for a transformational deed. Conversely, "kruthagna" reflects a situation where an individual forgets or fails to recognize the reason behind their initial expression of thanks.

This word signifies a complex human tendency. Often, as time passes or due to several other influences, the memory or acknowledgment of the transformative act might fade. It's as though the significance of the action becomes a little blurred or diluted in memory, leading to a disconnect between the gratitude initially felt and the present acknowledgment of it.

It would be best if you practiced Kruthagnjya every single day in order to have a happy and successful life. You may sit down with your eyes closed the moment you wake up and think about everything that has happened right in your life. Extend your "Kruthagnjatha" from the bottom of your heart to the God that you worship. The definition of God might not be the same for everybody. For some, it could have a face, and for some, it could be just an energy. No matter what it is, the moment you express your Kruthagnjyatha, the energy or God takes it and distributes it into the lives of your well-wishers, making life a blissful experience for everyone.

I am always thankful (krithagnjya) to all the women in my life. Eighty percent of the staff in our hospital are female. Women are treated differently everywhere. I wanted to break that age-old stereotype. We ensured that we hired more female staff and provided them an opportunity to grow. Their duty is not just to manage the house and hold the family together. It transcends beyond the world's preset frame. If you look at my personal journey, you can see how my mother, my wife, and Dr. Sangita have helped me transform into a better person.

Women play a phenomenal role in the development of the whole world. With the support and influence of a woman, you can go places. The language that we speak is called the mother tongue and not the father tongue. She is the best guru you will ever have.

You're in this world because your mother agreed to go through all the pain. Only a woman can multitask perfectly. She plays different roles every single day without complaining and without getting tired of it.

She can be a great daughter, a loving wife, an amazing mother, an outstanding employee, a responsible doctor or nurse, and whatnot! Her Dharma changes with every changing role. We often praise Artificial Intelligence a lot, but the truth is that our women already work like AI. They have built-in AI technology. A mother standing in the kitchen will know when her child moves too close to the edge of the verandah or toward the edge of the bed. She doesn't have to see them directly.

This is why, in South Indian philosophy, women are often addressed as Meenakshi. You must be aware of the Madurai Meenakshi Temple. But do you know the significance of the word in a global context? Meena means fish, and Akshi means eye. So, how do we relate it with women, or what is so specific about the eyes of a fish? Let me explain it to you. A fish doesn't have eyelids, which apparently means they never close their eyes. And that is how a mother is. She never even blinks when her child is awake.

When you visit Meenakshi temple, next time, look at the goddess from a different perspective – look at her as a woman who never blinks her eyes and keeps staring at her kids. We are her children.

Our Rishis treated women with respect and admiration during the Vedic period. Unfortunately, as time passed, we lost this Indic vision.

If you look at Devi Mahatmyam, it says, "Ya Devi Sarva Bhutheshu, Sarva Kariyeshu Sarvatha Namastasye Namastasye Namastasye Namo Namaha.

It means, "Oh, Devi, your presence is felt in every Karya (every work of mine).

Ya Devi Sarva Bhutheshu, (kshudha Rupena Samsthita), Namastasye Namastasye Namastasye Namo Namaha.

This means, "Oh, Devi, you are the embodiment of my Kshudha, (which means hunger)." Devi knows when you are hungry. A mother knows when her child is hungry. A newborn baby would never say, "Mom, I'm starving." She knows it and feeds the child.

Ya devi sarva bhuteshu, vidya rupena samsthita, Namastasye Namastasye Namastasye Namo Namaha

"Oh, Devi. Your presence is felt in the letter that I read. You're the source of all knowledge."

Ya devi sarva bhuteshu, Vruttir rupena samsthita, Namastasye Namastasye Namastasye Namo Namaha- "Oh Devi, you enable me to work and perform well at my workspace, your presence is felt everywhere."

This is how Veda has described women everywhere. This is what I grew up listening to, and I can undoubtedly say the women in my life have created a lasting impact. The moment you accept them as your influences, your dull life becomes colorful. Just because a woman is one foot shorter than a man or drinks less alcohol doesn't make her worth any less. This is something I teach everyone.

I would say time and again that women are the best teachers. While the whole world is your gurukul and every tiny creature on the planet, starting from an ant to humans to the sky and stars you see, is your guru, the influence of women remains eternal. While emphasizing the significance of women, it's essential to note that the value of men is in no way diminished. Both genders are equally important; it's just that women often showcase remarkable abilities that command more appreciation than we usually care to give them.

CONCLUSION

In penning this book, I aim to provide solace, guidance, and perspective to those who feel trapped in life's adversities. It's a compass for those who may have stumbled in their educational journey, faltered in their early career, or faced societal ridicule, mirroring many phases of my own life. It serves as a reminder that even in the face of seemingly insurmountable challenges, there is a path forward.

With age comes the gift of reflection. And as I stand at the threshold of my 60s, I see the vast landscape of my life, woven with threads of failures and successes, despair and hope. From being the subject of mockery to rising above it all, I've traversed a challenging path. Yet, it was the constant guidance from mentors and the resilience within that eventually led me to where I am today.

It deeply saddens me to witness the increasing number of young individuals succumbing to the pressure, taking drastic measures over circumstances that might appear minor to the external world. In my position in the healthcare sector, I've had a close vantage point to these heart-wrenching incidents. Conversations with grieving families often reveal triggers as trivial as academic ranks, harsh words from a loved one, or unrequited affections.

I hope this book serves as a beacon of hope to anyone grappling with life's lows. Every chapter is an assurance that setbacks can be stepping stones to success, and despair can give way to renewed hope, provided we maintain perspective and seek support.

In witnessing these heart-wrenching tales firsthand, a profound urge stirred within me. I felt compelled to reach out and make a difference in some way. The intent behind penning this book was to light a beacon of hope for the youth who might currently be standing where I once stood – at the crossroads of despair. My own journey was fraught with turmoil, but with the right guidance, support, and introspection, I found my peace. If this book prevents even a single individual from feeling trapped and taking that irreversible step, I'd consider it a triumph.

To all the parents reading this: your role is paramount. This book is not just a resource for the youth but also an essential guide for you. Your child might face adversities, but arming them with the right mindset is the first step towards ensuring they can navigate life's challenges. The tools and insights shared here aim to equip them not just for success, but more importantly, for happiness and peace.

To all the educators, mentors, and guides: recognize that every setback a young individual faces can be turned into a stepping stone, and your guidance can make all the difference.

To all the young souls out there: failures and setbacks are merely chapters in your life story. Do not let them define your entire narrative. Embrace them, learn from them, and use them as a foundation to build an even brighter future.

Life, when viewed with the right lens, can be as beautiful as a rose garden, complete with its thorns. It's all about navigating the tough patches and blossoming in the end. True success isn't easy, but it's absolutely worth the journey.

Wishing you all a journey filled with growth, happiness, and unparalleled success

ABOUT THE AUTHOR

Subramanyam Yadavalli's journey from humble beginnings to the helm of one of the world's premier hospitals – Apollo Hospitals, is a testament to his resilience, determination, and unwavering commitment to excellence. His remarkable ascent began as a ward boy in a diagnostic center, where he embarked on his extraordinary trajectory in the healthcare industry.

Throughout his career, he encountered myriad challenges and obstacles, each serving as a stepping stone towards his ultimate destination. From the corridors of the diagnostic center to the boardrooms of Apollo Hospitals, he absorbed invaluable lessons at every turn, transforming setbacks into opportunities for growth and learning.

His journey to the pinnacles of management excellence began with his post-graduate studies in Management, laying the foundation for his illustrious career. However, his thirst for knowledge and quest for mastery led him to pursue numerous management courses from prestigious institutions around the globe.

From Berkeley in the USA to Singapore Management University, from the esteemed Indian Institutes of Management (IIM) in Ahmedabad and Bangalore to the Indian School of Business (ISB) and Kellogg University, his academic pedigree is nothing short of remarkable.

His holistic approach to management truly sets him apart, blending his expertise in marketing, operations, and strategy with a profound understanding of Indian and Western philosophies.

Delving deep into the realms of Indic philosophy, he sought wisdom from various gurus and rishis in India, enriching his perspective and imbuing his leadership with a unique blend of ancient wisdom and modern management principles.

Beyond his corporate role, his passion for sharing knowledge extends to the realm of academia. As a visiting faculty member at various prestigious institutes, he imparts his wealth of experience and insights to the next generation of leaders, shaping the future of management education.

www.ingramcontent.com/pod-product-compliance
Lightning Source LLC
Chambersburg PA
CBHW031942070426
42450CB00005BA/414